Other Books by Clifford Goldstein

One Nation Under God
Between the Lamb and the Lion
The Remnant
Day of the Dragon
A Pause for Peace
False Balances
How Dare You Judge Us, God
1844 Made Simple
The Saving of America
Bestseller (The Clifford Goldstein story)

CHILDREN
OF THE
PROMISE

You can have the assurance of salvation!

CLIFFORD
GOLDSTEIN

Pacific Press Publishing Association
Boise, Idaho
Oshawa, Ontario, Canada

Cover photo by Mick Roessler/Super Stock
Edited by B. Russell Holt

Copyright © 1997 by
Pacific Press Publishing Association
Printed in the United States of America
All Rights Reserved

Accuracy of all quotations and references is the
responsibility of the author.

Goldstein, Clifford, 1953-
    Children of the promise : you can have the
assurance of salvation / Clifford Goldstein.
        p.   cm.
    ISBN 0-8163-1356-3 (pbk. : alk. paper)
    1. Regeneration (Theology) 2. Seventh-day
Adventists—Doctrines. I. Title.
BX6154.G615 1997
234'.4—dc20   96-9737
                                                  CIP

97 98 99 00 01 · 5 4 3 2 1

1

A gentle mist, mixed with the pungent smoke of breakfast fires, diffused and cooled the dawn light that awoke a river of blinking pink eyes. The missionary hurried along the stone path beside the Ganges, knowing that before long sunlight would incinerate the scene. Suddenly, he came to a rocky crest above the water where a young Hindu woman, softened by the haze, sat with a beautiful newborn infant asleep in her lap while a pitifully retarded boy of three shrieked like an animal as he pulled on her arm. The mother stared straight ahead, oblivious to the river of eyes blinking up at her, to the missionary's faint shadow that touched her as he walked by, and to the cries of the child, which the mist carried in the missionary's ears long after the woman had passed out of his sight.

Later that day, as the sun was setting and shadows of night reached up from the earth, the missionary returned. Before reaching the same spot, he recognized the child's cry. To his amazement, the mother was still sitting where he had left her; now, though, she had only the retarded boy, who twisted and whined in her arms. Instead of staring over the river, she peered down into the water, which no longer winked up at her, but in its inky darkness was closed, unanswering, inaccessible. The missionary noticed something wrong. Fearing the worst, he finished his approach and, hesitantly, asked what had happened.

She didn't respond, but stared into the black, silent water. Then, her wasted and strained face looked up and, her cheeks scarred by dirty tears, she answered, "I don't know about the gods in your country, but the gods in mine demand the best."

For thousands of years, the "gods" have demanded the best—and, for just as long, humans have faithfully responded. Mothers have thrown their babies into the bellies of beasts, into the mouths of volcanoes, and into the eyes of rivers that devoured them with one blink—all in order to be just before their gods. People have ripped out the hearts of their sons or have turned their virgin daughters into ashes on altars—all to be just before their gods. The faithful have beaten,

Clifford Goldstein

bruised, and broken themselves with whips, chains, and rods—all, again, to be just before their gods.

Ever since Cain's lame "fruit of the ground" oblation (Genesis 4:3), people have offered sacrifices to greedy deities who eventually asked not just for the fruit of their vineyards, but for the fruit of their wombs as well. Yet the madhouse of cries uttered from every burned child, from every strip of torn flesh, from every life sacrificed, never atoned for a single transgression, never made a single soul just with God, because only one way exists to be just before God—and that is through faith in Jesus Christ.

And the experience is called being *born again*.

2

In the middle of this century, among the swelling hills and fertile farms around Walton, New York, a boy was born. His name was Leonard, Leonard Orr.

It hadn't been an easy entrance. A breach baby, poor Leonard almost went straight from the womb to the grave.

But birth only began his troubles. Leonard's mother had been nearing the age when women think about osteoporosis and estrogen treatments, not prenatal care and maternity dresses, and she did not want the baby. When still too young to understand the juicy details, Leonard understood enough to know that he had been unwanted, an intruder barging in twelve years after his mother had decided that three girls were enough. Thus, nurtured on bitter breast milk that left a bad taste in his mouth long after he had spit out the nipple, the man sought to heal the pain inherited from the boy.

Eventually Leonard got involved in various New-Age philosophies, including Werner Erhard's est organization. Then, in 1962, while taking a bath, Leonard remained in the tub about two hours before regaining the strength to get out. Those few hours changed his life. In his bath water, he experienced something he later developed into "rebirthing."

Rebirthing theory goes like this: You're submerged in bath water while breathing through a snorkel. Then, from a series of breathing exercises, you regress to birth and even prenatal experiences. During the process, you relive physiologically, psychologically, and spiritually the moment of your first breath and thus are released from all the stress associated with being born. Only as you are freed from the trauma of your birth, the theory states, can you heal unresolved issues of your subconscious mind.

"Rebirthing," says a promotional brochure, "has the potential to bring you whatever you want. It's your choice." Among its touted benefits are increased health, improved relationships, easier conceptions and births, support during times of transition (marriage, divorce, career change, moving), and "awareness of Self as creator of life's scenarios."

Children of the Promise

Since the first professionally guided rebirth in a northern California hot tub almost twelve years after Leonard's first experience, rebirthing has multiplied into a multimillion-dollar business, including two major centers that train rebirthers. More than one hundred thousand professional rebirthers have guided 10 million people worldwide through the process.

Of course, the enemy of souls doesn't fret if 10 million or 100 million people get rebirthed. He's not concerned if people want to regress to a prenatal state and relive the trauma of their nativity. It's fine if endless multitudes, submerged in a bathtub, breathe through snorkels until they're literally blue in the face. He's happy that the process strengthens their relationships, improves their health, helps them in transitions, and gives them a greater "awareness of Self as creator of life's scenarios."

He doesn't even care how often anyone is rebirthed, just as long as none are ever born again.

3

Adherents of an Indian sect wear scarves across their mouths to prevent them from accidentally swallowing bugs. After all, a gnat might be the latest reincarnation of Mother.

The Tibetan Dalai Lama was chosen after religious leaders were convinced from oracles, miracles, and other signs that he was the reincarnation of his dead predecessor.

The Venda tribe of South Africa believes that when a person dies, the soul hovers over the tomb before seeking to be reborn in either human, mammalian, or reptilian form.

Though manifested in innumerable ways, for millennia millions have believed that after death the soul is reborn into a new life, human or otherwise. Hinduism, Buddhism, Sikhism, Shamanism, Jainism, along with forms of ancient Persian, Egyptian, and Greek religions, all teach (or taught) that after death the soul is reborn. Pythagoras and Plato believed that death is part of cyclical rebirths. Early Christian offshoots such as Manichaeism and Gnosticism, even Cabalistic Judaism, embraced reincarnation in one form or another. Today, New Ageism often encompasses the same concepts.

Perhaps humans so readily clutch these fanciful notions of new birth because they're so unhappy with what their first birth brought them. Returning as a dove, a dog, or even a gnat would be deemed a hopeful prospect for untold millions hoveled in misery.

Human life, this spasm of cellular metabolism, carries with it bereavement, starvation, disease, famine, war, disappointment, poverty, depression, alienation, emptiness, fear, insanity, child abuse, deformity, murder, etc. Unhappiness is so common that the *Journal of Medical Ethics* published an article called "A Proposal to Classify Happiness as a Psychiatric Disorder," which stated that happiness was "statistically abnormal, consists of a discrete cluster of symptoms, is associated with a range of cognitive abnormalities, and probably reflects the abnormal functioning of the central

Clifford Goldstein

nervous system."

Yet, even in their misery, most people prefer life to death, their worst foe. Thus reincarnation offers an alternative: you don't really die, you just change from one life form to another (one hopes) more pleasant one.

"Pitiful race of a day," wrote an ancient Greek dramatist, "children of accidents and sorrow, why do you force me to say what is better left unheard? The best of all is unobtainable—not to be born, to be nothing. The second best is to die early."

Or, perhaps, return as something else . . . ?

Science fiction writer H. G. Wells wrote: "A frightful queerness has come to life. Hitherto events have been held together by a certain logical consistency as the heavenly bodies have been held together by the golden cord of gravitation. Now it is as if that cord had vanished and everything is driven anyhow, anywhere, at a steadily increasing velocity. The writer is convinced that there is no way out or around or through the impasse. This is the end."

Unless, of course, you're reincarnated.

The point is simple: humanity's misery, traceable, no doubt, to the Fall, has given us, consciously or unconsciously, a desire for a new birth. This desire, though, has left people wide open to innumerable errors. Fortunately, despite these counterfeits, the Holy Spirit can use this desire to lead people to the *true* new birth, the one spoken of by Jesus when he said, "You must be born again" (John 3:7).

4

Born again?

A book about *that?* Most Adventists rarely utter the phrase, much less read (or write) tomes on the topic. It's not part of our vernacular, like "the truth," the "Spirit of Prophecy," or "the remnant."

Born again?

Is that something Adventists even do? The concept is usually associated with holy rollers shouting amid a fluster of tongues-speaking, miraculous "healings," and prostrate bodies "slain in the spirit,"—not with Seventh-day Adventists yawning through Sabbath School and church, where you might hear the prayer: "If any spark of a 'born-again' experience is kindled in this congregation,

Children of the Promise

O Heavenly Father, water that spark!"

Born-again Seventh-day Adventists? Sounds almost like Punk Rock Amish.

In one sense, our reticence is understandable. After all, who hasn't been born again these days? Tens of millions of Americans—football players, Watergate felons, movie stars making R-rated flicks, mass murderers, even politicians—all claim to have been born again. (Saying you've been born again has also become an unofficial requisite for the highest elected office in America.) For a while, the born-again thing was more faddish than green hair.

After being gunned down and crippled, Larry Flynt, the man who took newsstand pornography to new lows with his *Hustler* magazine, professed to have been born again—converted by Ruth Carter Stapleton, also born again. Yet Flynt never quit putting *Hustler* on the newsstands. Ronald Reagan said that he had been born again, yet he still allowed Nancy to plan his meetings and press conferences based on astrological charts!

No wonder we're leery.

Or even worse. The phrase *born again* conjures up more negativity among some Adventists than does "Mega-dittoes, Rush!" among the Democrats. Many link the new birth with legalism, fanaticism, repression, guilt, and lack of assurance in Christ—a perception strengthened because often the only Adventists

Clifford Goldstein

harping on the new birth anymore are right-wingers who usually turn it into another legalistic and perfectionistic standard of righteousness one must reach in order to be good enough to be saved.

How tragic that a person can attend Seventh-day Adventist schools from cradle roll to advanced degree programs and never know what *born again* means, much less experience it themselves. Meanwhile, among many evangelicals, being born again is the center of their Christian experience. They might not know about the Sabbath or unclean foods, but if born again, they have something more precious than going to church on the right day or not eating oysters.

Born again?

Jesus compared it to the wind: "The wind blows where it wishes, and you hear the sound of it, but cannot tell where it comes from and where it goes. So is everyone who is born of the Spirit" (John 3:8). Yet this is so subjective, so supernatural, mystical, and experiential—and Seventh-day Adventists don't tend to be that way.

Instead, we're *doctrinally* orientated. We need it in writing. *Verse, text, reference, please.* We distrust the ethereal, we're suspicious of the subjective. We have developed a complete system of objective truth (unrivaled, really, by any other church)—cosmological, ontological, theological, soteriological, and eschatological truth—all neatly wrapped with enough logic to make Christianity as sensible and reasonable as possible for minds that still "see through a glass, darkly" (1 Corinthians 13:12). We want things that can be analyzed, studied on a committee, and voted on, none of which a born-again experience easily lends itself to.

And, of course, we have these truths, concisely summarized in the *Twenty-Seven Fundamental Beliefs*. With twenty-seven fundamentals, what else do we need?

The answer's simple.

We need to be born again.

5

It's too bad about the negativity many feel toward the new birth. After all, generic Christianity, without being born again, is bad enough—but *Adventism* without it . . . ?

To be an Adventist, but not be born again, is to be mired in a depressing spiritual wasteland. The Ten Commandments, the Spirit of Prophecy, and the twenty-seven fundamentals become a never-ending labyrinth of rules, regulations, and unreachable standards that lead only to hopelessness and anger. There's no worse church to be in and not be born again. Better to be married to someone you don't love than to be a Seventh-day Adventist born only once.

On the other hand, to be a born-again Seventh-day

Children of the Promise

Adventist (patience—you'll get used to the phrase) is to be married, not only to the one you love, but to the one who has the most to offer. You can't, if born again, sign your name on the books of a better church. The burdens become joys, the rules privileges, and the standards expressions of love, because a born-again experience takes Christianity out of the head alone and puts it in the heart as well. And—for a religion in which the two central tenets are "Thou shalt love the Lord thy God with all thy heart, and with all thy soul, and with all thy mind. . . . [and] thy neighbour as thyself" (Matthew 22:37, 39)—the heart's where it ought to be too.

Someone once asked John Wesley why he preached so many sermons on the new birth. "Because," he answered, "you must be born again."

That includes Seventh-day Adventists as well.

First, a born-again experience can turn cold, dead, legalistic works into a vibrant, living, loving relationship with Jesus Christ.

Second, when a person is born again, obedience—rather than bondage (which is why people don't obey), becomes the most poignant and satisfying means of expressing our freedom in the Lord.

Finally, a born-again experience is the cure for a lack of assurance of salvation, because it *is* the experience of salvation.

We're not talking doctrines, rules, or knowledge.

Clifford Goldstein

We're talking a supernatural experience, a manifestation of the power of God working upon a human heart to change it from self-centeredness to God-centeredness. We're talking about the experience of going from death to life, from condemnation to justification, from damnation to salvation, from sin to holiness, from alienation to reconciliation. We're talking about being "born, not of blood, nor of the will of the flesh, nor of the will of man, but of God" (John 1:13)—something all the rules, forms, creeds, and doctrines can't do for you. You can no more make yourself be born the second time than you could the first.

The only difference? You had no choice the first time; you do the second.

6

When Jesus told Nicodemus that he must be "born again," the Pharisee's response—"How can a man be born when he is old? Can he enter the second time into his mother's womb, and be born?" (John 3:4)—sounded like Al Capone in the late stages of neurosyphilis, not like a spiritual leader of God's true church.

Which just goes to show: even a devout, diligent, and faithful Bible teacher can be devoid of the fundamental experience of salvation, that of being born again.

Now, from pillaging villages to bombing pubs, from performing abortions to shooting those who do, a profession of Christianity no more makes you

Christian than a profession of belief in God makes you divine. Creeds, forms, doctrines, even right ones, in and of themselves, can lead to death—and not just for those who follow them. Christ's greatest enemies so strictly adhered to the forms of religion that, in defense of those forms, they hung Him on a cross.

Nicodemus epitomized religious forms. He followed the rabbinic prohibitions that forbade thirty-nine types of Sabbath work, such as sewing two stitches, separating two threads, weaving two threads, writing two letters, or striking with a hammer. Nicodemus would swallow vinegar on the Sabbath, but not gargle with it. He would eat an egg laid on the seventh day, but only if the chicken who laid it was later killed (for having broken the Sabbath). On Sabbath, Nicodemus would not eat fruit taken from the ground because it might have fallen from the tree that day. He wouldn't even put out a house fire on *Shabbat*, except to save a life.

Ellen White wrote that Nicodemus was "a strict Pharisee, and prided himself on his good works. He was widely esteemed for his benevolence and his liberality in sustaining the temple service, and he felt secure of the favor of God" (*The Desire of Ages*, 171).

How many are deluded by their religiosity and good works into believing that they're secure in the favor of God? Who—because they were sprinkled as infants or immersed as adults—are convinced that they are therefore saved? How many who adhered to a creed, prayed, confessed their sins, went to the church (even the right one)—will hear the words, "I never knew you: depart from me, ye that work iniquity" (Matthew 7:23).

The issue isn't knowledge, piety, or a holy life. Nicodemus had all these. Unlike some of the snakes on the Sanhedrin, he wasn't vile, greedy, or contemptuous; he wasn't vain, ambitious, or hateful; he wasn't sinister, conniving, or self-serving—he just wasn't born again.

7

Born again?

In 1905, a twenty-six-year-old failed teacher working in a Swiss patent office published in the *Annalen der Physik* a nine-thousand-word paper titled "On the Electrodynamics of Moving Bodies," and humanity never looked at the world the same again. With his Special Theory of Relativity, the young Albert Einstein showed that time and space, far from being absolute, were relative, and that both would contract at high speeds until, at the speed of light, matter would shrink to nothing and time would stop. In other words, the faster a system moved, the slower a hypothetical clock attached to that system would tick until, at the speed of light, it would stop ticking completely—not because of any physical properties of the clock, but because of the properties of time itself!

However much Einstein's paper was, as the *Times* of London said, "an affront to common sense," it showed that our common *senses*—sight, sound, touch, taste, feel—are more limited than previously thought. Even time itself, supposedly absolute, steady, and constant (a premise of Newtonian physics), wasn't what it appeared to be.

From the sixth century B.C., when the Greeks first began to seek rational explanations for physical phenomena, humans have grappled with their limited ability to perceive the natural world. Our receptors— eyes, ears, skin—are blunt, even crude in comparison to what's really out there. It's like we're stuck using a thumb to understand the details of a small Swiss watch.

For example, some insects can smell other ones a mile away, when we can't smell them even if they crawl up our noses! Dogs can hear sounds that make them jump, when we hear nothing. Our noses, our ears, are too insensitive, too dull to discern some smells and sounds just as real, just as much a part of the physical world as are the tunes of Alice Cooper or the fragrances of Calvin Kline perfumes.

Even our eyes, the most powerful, precise, and sensitive instruments for relaying data to the mind, limit us to a very narrow slice of the electromagnetic spec-

Clifford Goldstein

trum. At one end, cosmic rays, a trillionth of a centimeter in wavelength, or on the other end, the longer infrared, radar, and television wavelengths, are all inaccessible to us in our natural state, yet these are as real as the slim electromagnetic band, which—for almost all human history—is all that our eyes have been able to detect.

Instruments—everything from microscopes to Geiger counters—by opening vistas once totally inaccessible to humans, show just how little our natural physiology allows us to perceive.

And even what we perceive often deceives us. When someone commented to Austrian philosopher Ludwig Wittgenstein about the ancients' stupidity for believing, before the Copernican revolution, that the sun circled around the earth, Wittgenstein responded: "I agree. But I wonder what the sun would have looked like if it *had* circled the earth."

Immanuel Kant, meanwhile, in his *Critique of Pure Reason*, argued that we can never know reality in and of itself, but can perceive it only as it is processed by our minds. Our understanding of the world is formed, structured, and limited by the forms, the structures, and limits of the brain, in the same sense that data entered into a computer is processed by the form, structure, and limits of the computer and the specific program running it. Though a reality exists independently of us, we can know it only as our senses take it in, and then only as our minds, already pre-programmed, process the data.

"Just as a person who wears rose-colored glasses," wrote Samuel Strumpf in explaining Kant, "sees everything in that color, so every human being, having the faculty of thought, inevitably thinks about things in accordance with the natural structure of the mind."

For this reason, it's utterly incomprehensible, both from an experiential (sense perception) and rational (mind structure) perspective that time doesn't always flow at a constant rate but can actually slow down or even stop. The concept of relativity is exceedingly difficult to understand, because it deals with something far beyond what our senses can perceive and what even our minds (Einstein's excepted) have been structured to process.

Meanwhile, whatever commonalities all human minds have, each brain is unique, and thus we all see, perceive, and understand reality somewhat differently. Pure objectivity is impossible from a human standpoint. Subjectivity starts, wrapped in our DNA, and then continually unfolds in the endless variables of upbringing, culture, education, and daily experience that make each of us exceptions.

How, could the *New York Times*, in an article about Federal Reserve Chairman Allen Greenspan (8 June 1995), run the headline, "Greenspan Sees Chance of Recession," while the *Wall Street Journal*–covering the same story, in the same city, the same day!—run the headline, "Fed Chairman Doesn't See Recession on the Horizon"? The answer is because humans are hopelessly subjective in the way they perceive and understand reality—the same reason why the *Wall Street Journal* (28 November 1995) could report, "Orders for Machine Tools Increased 45.5% in October," while the *New York Times*, covering the same story, the same day, in the same city, could report, "Machine-Tool Orders Dropped 29% In October." Something happened to machine tool orders in October. The problem is the subjective, imperfect manner in which humans *perceived* it.

Also, if we can't even accurately grasp and understand physical realities, how much less spiritual ones, those not even belonging to what we understand as the material world. Angels and demons, though hidden from our senses, are as much a part of reality as the germs we inhale. The Holy Spirit circles the planet, as real as the wind, yet the limitations God has placed on our perceptions, and the way He has construed our minds, has made the Spirit completely inaccessible to our sight, taste, and touch, though He exists all around us, even in an intimate way. Scientific gadgetry allows us to detect things that our eyes and ears never will, but what instrument will ever recognize the motion of angels or measure the influence of the Holy Spirit, which are just as real as cosmic rays or high-pitched sounds?

All around us, a physical and spiritual reality exists that we, in our natural state, can't perceive. Isolated by our senses, limited by the processes of our minds, we are trapped within ourselves, grasping at the world that surrounds us, just as severe myopics do at the blur that surrounds them.

Fortunately, the Lord has provided a means to help us focus, not just on spiritual realities, but (in a different sense) even on physical realities as well. God wants to give us a clearer, crisper, finer perception of both the seen and unseen. And He does it for us after we, guided by His Word, are born again.

8

In a posthumous compilation of essays (*Ethics*), theologian-martyr Dietrich Bonhoeffer repeatedly referred to two Bible verses: "For by him were all things created, that are in heaven, and that are in earth, visible and invisible, whether they be thrones, or dominions, or principalities, or powers: all things were created by him, and for him: And he is before all things, and by him all things consist" (Colossians 1:16, 17).

Whatever their theological implications, these texts contain a key metaphysical one: ultimate reality, hence ultimate truth (for what is truth other than knowing reality?) can be understood only in relationship to Jesus Christ. If all things were created by, and for, Jesus Christ, and if by Christ all things exist, then all things—i.e. ultimate reality—can never be understood apart from Him. In Christ "we live, and move, and have our being" (Acts 17:28). It doesn't get more basic than that.

"The reality of Christ," wrote Bonhoeffer, "comprises the reality of the world within itself. The world has no reality of its own, independent of the revelation of God in Christ. . . . The world, like all created things, is created through Christ and with Christ as its end, and consists in Christ alone (John 1:10; Col. 1:16). To speak of the world without speaking of Christ is empty and abstract. The world is relative to Christ, whether it knows it or not."

But the world *doesn't* know it, and that's its problem. If truth exists in Jesus Christ alone, then apart from Him—where most people are—only disharmony, ignorance, and pain can result.

And no wonder. Every gift has been perverted and abused—speech (we lie), sex (we make porno), sight (we covet), imagination (we devise evil)—until our small, frail human gears are so out of sync with reality that they grind against it.

Also, think how totally alienated from reality, how far removed from the basis of their existence, are those whose worldview is based on evolution. They might as well believe that the stork brought them. Imagine the darkness that must enshroud those unaware that the

Clifford Goldstein

One in whom we "live, and move, and have our being" even exists! Those without knowledge of the Holy Spirit and angels are as out of touch with true reality as were the ancients who believed in a geocentric universe with a flat, stationary earth. People who have never experienced the fundamental principle of all existence, that "God is love," have their faces chained to the inner wall of a cave. And, saddest of all—to never know the reality of what Christ accomplished on the cross is, merely, to exist, not to live. No wonder Jesus said, "Let the dead bury their dead" (Matthew 8:22).

Yet the new birth, enhanced and guided by the Word, changes all that. Being born again doesn't open people to every truth or physical reality. They don't suddenly smell bugs, hear high-pitched whistles, or become deep theologians understanding "all mysteries, and all knowledge" (1 Corinthians 13:2). Instead, the new birth helps them attain an awareness of truths that those without it can never fully have. It brings existence, both seen and unseen, into sharper focus.

Reality exists in Christ, but it encompasses truths far beyond our intellect, truths that must be experienced to be understood. And here's where the new birth comes in—because it helps us grasp reality.

And that reality is that Jesus Christ is the Creator and Redeemer. You can believe that Christ has created and redeemed you, but that belief alone will never bring you into harmony with truth. Only the new birth can. It resynchronizes our gears to fit reality.

Being born again, then, is the means by which God makes the truth about Jesus Christ—and all that it entails—a personal, intimate experience. That's why Jesus said, "You must be born again." It's the only way that ultimate reality—the truth of Jesus Christ as Creator, Sustainer, and Redeemer—can become real for those He created and redeemed.

9

Born again?

I was sitting in a Santa Fe cafe on a cool May day reading political philosophy and drinking a bowl of decaf cappuccino topped with whipped cream and cinnamon when a young man, catching the title of my book, stopped at my table. I invited him to sit and immediately turned the discussion to spiritual things.

He expressed disbelief in God and, as the conversation continued, I said: "Though nature testifies to the existence of a Creator, I can't say that it necessarily witnesses to anything *distinctly* Christian."

My words bothered me for days. Shouldn't creation affirm something distinctly Christian? After all, Christianity is *the* truth. It—not Hinduism, Islam, or

Children of the Promise

Buddhism—is *the* explanation for reality, nature, and natural law. Existence comes from Christ alone, "For by him were all things created, that are in heaven, and that are in the earth, visible and invisible, whether they be thrones, or dominions, or principalities, or powers: all things were created by him, and for him: and he is before all things, and by him all things consist" (Colossians 1:16, 17). Shouldn't all things "created by Him" testify to Him alone and no other? Why doesn't nature proclaim specifically Christian doctrine—as opposed to Islamic, Jewish, or Hindu doctrine, all of which include belief in a Creator? Shouldn't creation witness *uniquely* to Christianity?

The answer came a few weeks later, from a sentence in a copy of *National Geographic*. "During early pregnancy," it read, "neurons can grow at a rate of 250,000 a minute."

Two hundred and fifty thousand neurons a minute! *That's more than four thousand a second.* Neurons are among the body's most complicated cells; each one contains fantastically baffling and intricate electrochemical processes. The world's greatest biologists and chemists couldn't produce one neural cell *wall* in fifty years, much less a single neuron itself, and yet *in vitro* more than four thousand of these are created per second (second!) without us understanding how it happens or consciously taking part in it at all.

Clifford Goldstein

Of course. How could anything we do possibly bridge the gap between us and the power that creates neurons at the rate of 4,000 per second? The power that holds subatomic particles in place and created and sustains a billion galaxies testifies to a God far beyond us and anything our pathetic little works could ever produce. How feeble our efforts as impure sinful beings must look to the God who could ignite and hurl a billion suns across the cosmos.

Nature, in all its awesome complexity, inaccessibility, and grandeur screams at the futility of salvation by works. Whether the burning image of the Pleiades in the night sky or the intricacies of mitochondrial functions in the simplest cell—reality mocks man's efforts to make himself acceptable enough to the One who spoke these things into existence. How could tossing your infant into a river, beating yourself with sticks, or even donating your money to the poor bridge the gap between you and the Creator who makes Hubble's deep-space photos seem like standing on the shore and throwing a rock in the Pacific? It's a joke, as ridiculous as if Hitler in his last days had tried to make amends by donating his spleen to a Jewish hospital.

And yet, that's just what all these other religions teach, one way or another. Either in this life, or in lives to come, you can make yourself good enough to be accepted by the God who implanted endless gen-

Children of the Promise

erations in a single seed. Despite the glaring evidence from every atom and every star, these faiths say that you can reconcile yourself to the Creator, that you can earn salvation by good works. In contrast, Christianity alone teaches, *Nothing you can do can make yourself good enough for God. All you can do is lean upon the merits of the Saviour, Jesus Christ, who, Himself the Creator, alone can bring salvation to man.*

The Bible says, "The heavens declare the glory of God" (Psalm 19:1) and nowhere was God's glory greater than at the cross, where Christ reconciled God to man and closed the chasm between them. At Calvary, what all nature testifies to, that man cannot save himself, was displayed in full. Man couldn't do it for himself, so Jesus Christ did.

"Neither is there salvation in any other: for there is none other name under heaven given among men, whereby we must be saved" (Acts 4:12). That's *no* other name under heaven, especially our own.

Of course, the creation of 4,000 neural cells a second doesn't automatically prove that "a man is justified by faith, without the deeds of the law" (Romans 3:28). But could it lead to the conclusion that all our attempts at salvation are futile, vain, pathetic—which then points to Christianity, the only faith that teaches our works are, indeed, futile, vain, and pathetic, the message of creation itself?

"Knowing that a man is not justified by the works

of the law, but by the faith of Jesus Christ, even we have believed in Jesus Christ, that we might be justified by the faith of Christ, and not by the works of the law: for by the works of the law shall no flesh be justified" (Galatians 2:16).

Paul here states in narrow terms what all creation states in broad ones, which is that we can't justify ourselves. "For by grace are ye saved through faith; and that not of yourselves: it is the gift of God: Not of works, lest any man should boast" (Ephesians 2:8, 9). In Christian theology, it's called "justification by faith," and not only is it based on the essential reality of the world, Christ as Creator and Redeemer, it's the only basis for the essential Christian experience as well, that of being born again.

10

How ironic that one of the greatest "born again" verses in Scripture never mentions the phrase! Instead, the supernatural new birth is best expressed by the legal and objective text: "There is therefore now no condemnation to them which are in Christ Jesus" (Romans 8:1).

What does that have to do with being born again?

After the Fall, Satan said that God could be just and punish man, or be merciful and forgive him—but not both. The Bible, though, describes God as both just and merciful: "Tell ye, and bring them near; yea, let them take counsel together: who hath declared this from ancient time? who hath told it from that time? have not I the Lord? and there is no God else beside me; a just God and a Saviour; there is none beside me" (Isaiah 45:21). "And the Lord passed by before him, and proclaimed, The Lord, the Lord God, merciful and gracious, longsuffering, and abundant in goodness and truth" (Exodus 34:6).

The answer, of course, is Calvary. Here God's mercy and justice reached a climax: His justice, because God's righteous judgment against sin was poured out in full—and mercy, because it was poured out in full on Jesus instead of on sinners. God's justice demanded that our sin be punished; His mercy that Jesus face the punishment in our stead.

"Now is the judgment of this world:" Jesus said right before the cross, "now shall the prince of this world be cast out. And I, if I be lifted up from the earth, will draw all men unto me" (John 12:31, 32).

Jesus Himself faced the judgment, the condemnation of our sins, so we don't have to (which, by the way, is how we get through the investigative judgment: when our names come up, we aren't condemned, because Jesus faced our condemnation at the cross).

"For he hath made him to be sin for us, who knew no sin; that we might be made the righteousness of God in him" (2 Corinthians 5:21).

"Christ hath redeemed us from the curse of the law, being made a curse for us: for it is written, Cursed is everyone that hangeth on a tree" (Galatians 3:13).

Children of the Promise

In *The Desire of Ages*, Ellen White wrote:

> Upon Christ as our substitute and surety was laid the iniquity of us all. He was counted a transgressor, that He might redeem us from the condemnation of the law. The guilt of every descendant of Adam was pressing upon His heart. The wrath of God against sin, the terrible manifestation of His displeasure because of iniquity, filled the soul of His Son with consternation.... Christ felt the anguish which the sinner will feel when mercy shall no longer plead for the guilty race. It was the sense of sin, bringing the Father's wrath upon Him as man's substitute, that made the cup He drank so bitter, and broke the heart of the Son of God (753).

At the cross, God proved He could be both "just, and the justifier of him which believeth in Jesus" (Romans 3:26). That's why there's "now no condemnation for those who are in Christ Jesus." The condemnation of any sin we have ever committed, or will ever commit, was already fulfilled at Calvary, and when we, by faith, accept Christ as Redeemer, what He completed for us provisionally becomes ours personally and experientially. And not only is our condemnation removed at the moment of conversion, but it's automatically replaced with the perfect righteousness of Christ.

Thus, the question is, Can we go from being condemned by God to eternal death for our sins, to having that condemnation removed and replaced with perfect righteousness of Christ, and not be transformed? Could a reversal of our legal standing before our Maker not change our lives?

Of course not. It's like a prisoner pardoned. Whatever the paper-shuffling involved in a government office miles from his cell, the result radically affects him. The pardon isn't just legal paperwork; it becomes a subjective experience in the prisoner's life: he walks away free. Though the pardon was accomplished outside and away from him, his life has been powerfully changed by it.

The same with us. When we're no longer condemned by God, our life changes, and that change—however personal, unique, and subjective—begins with the new birth.

11

Just before his death, a poet was asked, "Have you made peace with the Lord?"

"I didn't realize," he quipped, "that we were at war."

What the bard didn't know was that, outside of Christ, he was, if not at war, at least at odds, with God.

"He that is not with me," Jesus said, "is against me" (Matthew 12:30).

"The carnal mind is enmity against God: for it is not subject to the law of God, neither indeed can be" (Romans 8:7).

"And you, that were sometime alienated and enemies in your mind by wicked works, yet now hath he reconciled" (Colossians 1:21).

We are, by nature, "the children of wrath"

Clifford Goldstein

(Ephesians 2:3). However well our parents may have programmed our software, we're still hard-wired in sin. Only Adam, Eve, and Jesus Christ came into the world pure and reconciled to the Father; everyone else drops in, if not guilty of Adam's fall, at least overcome by its consequences, which is our own sin and the alienation, separation, and enmity it brings.

"Wherefore, as by one man sin entered into the world, and death by sin; and so death passed upon all men, for that all have sinned" (Romans 5:12).

Yet God doesn't take sin lightly, ours or anyone else's. "For the wrath of God is revealed from heaven against all ungodliness and unrighteousness of men" (Romans 1:18). Iniquity has alienated us from the Lord ("being alienated from the life of God" (Ephesians 4:18), separated us from Him ("your iniquities have separated between you and your God" Isaiah 59:2), and made us enemies ("For if, when we were enemies . . ."–Romans 5:10). Sin, and the sad consequences thereof, are our only birthright.

Which leads directly to another born-again text: "And all things are of God, who hath *reconciled us* to himself by Jesus Christ" (2 Corinthian 5:18, emphasis supplied).

Though Christ's death brought the world itself back into God's favor (2 Corinthians 5:19), only those who have chosen to accept Christ are truly reconciled to Him in the sense of salvation. This reconciliation necessitates a personal commitment to God through a union of the soul with Jesus Christ. Only then does the alienation, enmity, and separation naturally wrought by sin vanish. By being reconciled to God through Christ—not only by what He has accomplished for us at the cross, but by His High Priestly ministry—the fellowship between God and man is restored. "For if, when we were enemies, we were reconciled to God by the death of His Son, much more, being reconciled, we shall be saved by His life" (Romans 5:10).

The good news is that once reconciled through Christ, an individual can have a relationship with God *almost* as if she had never sinned. *Almost*, because the emotional, physical, spiritual, and intellectual devastation of sin hinders our capacity to fully relate to Christ as Adam no doubt did before the Fall. Nevertheless, by God's act of reconciliation, every barrier has been broken between the Creator and His human creatures. Through Jesus Christ, we can enjoy communion with God. Nothing but our own shortcomings, doubts, and iniquity can block this fellowship.

"Having therefore, brethren, boldness to enter into the holiest by the blood of Jesus, By a new and living way, which he hath consecrated for us, through the veil, that is to say, his flesh: And having a high priest over the house of God; Let us draw near with a true heart in full assurance of faith" (Hebrews 10:19-22).

Can a person, alienated from God but now suddenly reconciled to Him, not experience a radical change in her life? It's like marriage. Could an estranged and alienated couple be reconciled and their lives not be affected?

How much more, then, being reconciled to God. Can someone separated from her Maker, but who is restored by Christ to a harmonious relationship with Him, not have a new existence? How can anyone, once estranged from God but now accepted in Him as perfect, not be changed?

The answer, simply, is that she can't.

12

Though hating Christianity, when he wrote that "the living are just a species of the dead," Frederich Nietzsche repeated an essential truth spoken by Christ, who said, "Let the dead bury their dead" (Matthew 8:22).

Who's dead, who's alive? The answer can be best understood in the context of the new-birth experience.

A few chapters after His conversation with Nicodemus, Jesus uttered a crucial born-again text: "Verily, verily, I say unto you, He that heareth my word, and believeth on him that sent me, hath everlasting life, and shall not come into condemnation; but is passed from death unto life" (John 5:24).

Clifford Goldstein

The New Testament is explicit: life exists only in Christ. Apart from Him, there might be breath, protoplasmic function, and sentience, but no real life.

"And this is the record, that God hath given to us eternal life, and this life is in his Son; He that hath the Son hath life; and he that hath not the Son of God hath not life" (1 John 5:11, 12).

As humans, we measure time in teaspoons, so two, twenty, fifty, even a hundred years of human existence is considered "life." But for Jesus, who sees across eternity better than we see across the next moment, our short span of mortal existence, this pitiful evanescence, isn't long enough even to qualify as "life." Finite time can't be contrasted against eternity; it doesn't even count. It's as if the old among us die at conception.

"For what is your life? It is even a vapor, that appeareth for a little time, and then vanisheth away" (James 4:14).

Of course, even those who have eternal life in Christ face carnal dissolution. Flesh inevitably fails. The "earthly house of this tabernacle" (2 Corinthians 5:1) dissolves. But is this real death?

"I am the resurrection and the life," Jesus said, "he that believeth in me, though he were dead, yet shall he live: And whosoever believeth in me shall never die" (John 11:25, 26).

Jesus taught that death is only a temporary sleep,

4—C.P.

not death in the true biblical sense, which is the eternal destruction that awaits the lost after the second resurrection. Just as mortal life is too short to qualify as true life, fleshly death is too short to qualify as true death—not in the face of everlasting destruction.

From God's perspective, for death to be death and for life to be life—they must be eternal; otherwise they're really neither.

Also, Jesus said that he who believes in him "shall not come into *condemnation*; but is passed from death unto life" (John 5:24, emphasis supplied). It's the removal of condemnation that makes a person pass from death to life, and this removal comes only to those who believe in Jesus. "He that believeth on him is not condemned: but he that believeth not is condemned already" (John 3:18).

Eternal life, then, begins with a legal action on the part of Christ in our behalf. We are given eternal life now. "Verily, verily, I say unto you, He that believeth on me *hath everlasting life*" (John 6:47, emphasis supplied). The moment we accept Jesus, we *have* eternal life in Him, probably because God knows that we will be resurrected to immortality after a sleep.

And though it's more a declaration than a biological transformation, at least for the present, this passage from death to life causes a radical transformation in a person's existence. How could it not? We exchange a swatch of life and an endless death for a swatch of death and an endless life. It's like a dying person suddenly being given a pill that saves his life. He gets up from bed and walks away, a radical difference from being dead.

How much more, then, we—going from eternal death to eternal life—will be changed as well?

13

In contrast to Paul's explicit expositions in Romans, Galatians, and Ephesians, not much gospel *theology* appears in the Gospels themselves. Of the four, John (chapter three) gives the clearest explanation, not only of the "good news," but of the new birth as well. No doubt, Jesus purposely linked the two.

"Verily, verily, I say unto thee, Except a man be born again, he cannot see the kingdom of God. . . . Verily, verily, I say unto thee, Except a man be born of water and the Spirit, he cannot enter into the kingdom of God. . . . Marvel not that I said unto thee, Ye must be born again" (John 3:3, 5, 7).

Nowhere else is the new birth so emphasized. It's not even mentioned again in the Gospels. Yet three times in this one chapter Jesus stressed the need to be "born again." According to Him, you can't be saved without it.

And you can't be saved without the gospel either, which is why, after chiding Nicodemus for his spiritual ignorance, Jesus immediately launched into His most complete explanation of the gospel.

"As Moses lifted up the serpent in the wilderness," Jesus said, "even so must the Son of man be lifted up: That whosoever believeth in him should not perish, but have eternal life" (John 3:14, 15).

Pointing to Calvary through the symbolism of the bronze serpent, Jesus taught justification by faith. Only by looking to Him will people live, just as those bitten by the serpents lived only when they looked to the bronze model. With the words "whosoever *believeth* in him" Jesus showed that faith alone, not works, is the means of appropriating "eternal life."

Next, in John 3:16, Jesus told of God's love for us—"For God so loved the world"—and His willingness to save us through "his only begotten Son." Unlike when Jesus talked about plucking out the eye, turning the cheek, or loving your neighbor as yourself, the emphasis here is on faith alone: "That whosoever *believeth* in him should not perish, but have everlasting life."

In verse 17—"For God sent not his Son into the world to condemn the world; but that the world through him might be saved"—the emphasis is upon God, whose love sent Jesus, and upon Jesus, through whom we have eternal life. Our response is to believe.

"He that believeth on him is not condemned: but he that believeth not is condemned already, because he hath not believed in the name of the only begotten Son of God" (John 3:18).

Jesus linked the need of the new birth to God's accomplishment of salvation through Christ. At first, this might seem like a mixed match. After all, one is the supernatural imprint of the Spirit upon a person's mind; the other is the legal, forensic act that Christ accomplished outside of humanity. One touches the innermost recesses of the soul; the other is a declaration of forgiveness in the far reaches of the universe. The first deals with the law being written on our hearts, the second with our names being written in heaven. One is an ongoing subjective experience in us; the other is the once-and-for-all objective sacrifice of Christ for us.

Yet Jesus linked the two, because what He has done *for us* will inevitably have an effect *in us*. And that effect is manifested as the new birth.

14

The gospel can be summarized in one word: righteousness. "For in the gospel a righteousness from God is revealed" (Romans 1:17, NIV). Yet for the monk Martin Luther, *righteousness* had been the most fearsome term in Scripture. Understanding it only as the Latin legal concept of a just punishment for evil deeds (*justitia*), Luther trembled in anticipation of one day facing that *righteousness*.

Eventually, the text—"Now the righteousness of God *without the law* is manifested, being witnessed by the law and the prophets" (Romans 3:21)—showed Luther that this righteousness wasn't achieved through obedience to the law, but was the righteousness of God Himself credited to the believer by grace.

Children of the Promise

A sinner can never earn enough righteousness to be saved, so God instead *declares* the sinner righteous. Luther understood this declaration as the basis of justification by faith, the essence not only of the Reformation, but of Christianity itself.

"Since we are sinful, unholy, we cannot perfectly obey the holy law," wrote Ellen White (*Steps to Christ*, 62).

> We have no righteousness of our own with which to meet the claims of the law of God. But Christ has made a way of escape for us. He lived on earth amid trials and temptations such as we have to meet. He lived a sinless life. He died for us, and now He offers to take our sins and give us His righteousness. If you give yourself to Him, and accept Him as your Saviour, then, sinful as your life may have been, for His sake you are accounted righteous. Christ's character stands in place of your character, and you are accepted before God just as if you had not sinned (62).

"Therefore we conclude that a man is justified by faith, without the deeds of the law" (Romans 3:28).

Justification is, technically, not to be "made worthy," but to be "accounted worthy," a crucial distinction, because whatever God ultimately does in us, our acceptance with Him must always be based upon what He has done for us. The Lord *declares* us worthy, which means that despite our sins, imperfections, and faults, God credits us with the perfect righteousness of Jesus Christ, who constantly applies the merits of that perfect righteousness in behalf of repentant sinners. In God's eyes, we are declared as righteous as Jesus Christ Himself.

Now, no voice from heaven declares "Justified!" nor does God stamp "Accounted worthy!" on our foreheads. Rather, to be declared righteous means that your name is written in the book of life—the official, legal record of your new status before God.

"Notwithstanding in this rejoice not, that the spirits are subject unto you," Jesus said, "but rather rejoice, because your names are written in heaven" (Luke 10:20). "At that time thy people shall be delivered, every one that shall be found written in the book" (Daniel 12:1). "Whosoever was not found written in the book of life was cast into the lake of fire" (Revelation 20:15).

Justification, therefore, includes our names being written in a book billions, if not trillions, of miles away, but only because of what happened at the cross more than 1,900 years ago. In both the time and space continuum, justification is separate from the believer. Something that happened almost 2,000 years ago, and who knows how many light years away, is, clearly, separate. But this way we can truly understand that justification is not our own work. We can no more justify ourselves, even by perfect obedience to the law, than we can write our names in heaven or, for that matter, go back to the cross.

On the other hand, Paul did write that, "Know ye not, that so many of us as were baptized into Jesus Christ, were baptized into his death? Therefore we are buried with him by baptism into death: that like as Christ was raised up from the dead by the glory of the Father, even so we should walk in newness of life" (Romans 6:3, 4). And Ellen White wrote that "heaven is much nearer to earth than we imagine, and we are nearer to heaven than we imagine" (*Sermons and Talks*, 200).

Which leads to this point: however legal, sterile, and distant justification is—a subjective, personal side to it exists, because justification happens to subjective, personal beings. When we accept what Christ did two thousand years ago, then somewhere in the universe our name is placed in the book of life. We are no longer condemned, alienated from God, or even (biblically) dead—and the freedom, the joy, and the release that results from this change in our status is so powerfully manifest in our lives that we are "born again."

The new birth is, essentially, the *experience* of justification by faith. It is *not* justification itself, which is always a work of God apart from us, but it is the inevitable, subjective result of that work, which will be manifested in us. When the minister pronounces you man and wife, you are married; when God declares you justified, you are "born again." They cannot be separated.

That's why Jesus linked His most explicit preaching of justification with His only recorded statements about the new birth. "You must be born again," He said—not because the new birth can save you (it can't)—but because you must be justified in order to be saved, and the new birth is the inevitable experience of that justification.

"Except a man be born again," Jesus said, "he cannot see the kingdom of God" (John 3:3).

With these thirteen simple words, Jesus dispelled the futility of mere external religion or intellectual assent to truth as a saving faith. Salvation, however much based on God's work for us, has to be made manifest as an experience in us, or we're really not saved.

"He has delivered us from the dominion of darkness and transferred us to the kingdom of his beloved Son, in whom we have redemption, the forgiveness of sins" (Colossians 1:13, 14, RSV).

"He destined us in love to be his sons through Jesus Christ, according to the purpose of his will, to the praise of his glorious grace which he freely bestowed on us in the Beloved. In him we have redemption through his blood, the forgiveness of our trespasses, according to the riches of his grace which he lavished upon us" (Ephesians 1:5-8, RSV).

"You, who were dead in trespasses and the uncircumcision of your flesh, God made alive together with him, having forgiven all our trespasses" (Colossians 2:13, RSV).

Redeemed by His blood; our trespasses forgiven. These might be heavenly transactions, but we experience the results on the earth. Through the cross, we are forgiven, made alive, reconciled, and accounted perfect before God. These transformations cannot happen and we not be radically changed, to the point that we have a new life. That's why Jesus called it being "born again," or literally, being born "from above" (*anothen*).

15

After the Civil War, Abraham Lincoln was asked how he would deal with the rebellious states. "I'll treat them," he said, "as if they had never left."

Justification by faith works the same way: God treats us as if we had never left, had never been condemned, had never been alienated from Him. We are as accepted in Him as was Jesus Christ, who "from the days of eternity . . . was one with the Father" (*The Desire of Ages*, 19).

If the new birth is the experience of justification by faith, then it also must be the experience of assurance with God, because the essence of justification is assurance.

"Therefore being justified by faith, we have peace

Children of the Promise

with God through our Lord Jesus Christ" (Romans 5:1). Paul bases peace with God on the foundation of justification by faith. There's no peace if there's no assurance, and assurance comes from being justified.

Peace with God, then—through assurance of salvation—is the first fruit of the new birth. To not only believe that your sins have been pardoned, but to experience that pardon, is the essence of being born again.

This truth can never be proven scientifically. Christian metaphysics isn't discovered in a lab; it can't be summarized in a mathematical formula. Only by experience can it be understood, and only those who have had this experience know the joy, the gratefulness, and the love that come from forgiveness of sins. Having surrendered themselves to God, having renounced any merit in themselves, having repented, confessed, and mourned—and, leaning totally upon the worth of Jesus Christ alone—they are enveloped in the robe of righteousness that they know has been woven on the loom of heaven. They enjoy full assurance of acceptance with God because in a powerful, intimate way, they have experienced that acceptance for themselves.

Of course, even born-again Christians don't always tingle with these warm fuzzies. In fact (unless we've accepted the curious doctrine of "once saved always saved"), we all might even struggle at times with

Clifford Goldstein

doubts about our salvation. None of us lives perfectly, and we occasionally question our standing with God.

However, having experienced acceptance in Christ through the new birth, we can rejoice in that acceptance even when, instead of feeling the gentle touch of heaven, we're choking on remorse and self-hatred. Claiming, and accepting for ourselves that "Christ died for the ungodly" (Romans 5:6), that "while we were yet sinners, Christ died for us" (Romans 5:8), and that "blessed is he whose transgression is forgiven, whose sin is covered" (Psalm 32:1), even when we cringe over our own filthiness, unworthiness, and evil, is as much a part of the salvation experience as when we hear angels gently whisper songs of love and acceptance in our ears.

If anything, the realization of our own unworthiness can be one of our best safeguards. The sense of our own sinfulness will keep us clinging to Christ and His righteousness, which alone bring the changes in us that are an inevitable result of the new-birth experience.

Paul's words, "Being confident of this very thing, that he which hath begun a good work in you will perform it until the day of Jesus Christ" (Philippians 1:6), apply to each "born again" Seventh-day Adventist. As long as we *choose* to maintain a saving relationship to Christ—which involves a continuous surrender our will to His—we must, by repentance and faith, believe that He will complete His work in us, just as He did in the thief on the cross, knowing, too, that we are accepted in Him as perfect.

Assurance in Christ is often a balance between believing God's promises of forgiveness and knowing that forgiveness in an intimate and personal manner.

Either way, or hovering somewhere in between, assurance is not only the essential new-birth experience, it's the basis from which everything else in that experience begins.

16

"Verily, verily, I say unto thee, Except a man be born again, he cannot see the kingdom of God. . . . Verily, verily, I say unto thee, except a man be born of water and of the Spirit, he cannot enter into the kingdom of God. . . . Marvel not that I said unto thee, Ye must be born again" (John 3:3, 5, 7).

The three times that Jesus stressed the necessity of being born again, His focus wasn't on justification, the foundation of the new birth, but on the subjective, supernatural experience itself.

The reason appears in chapter 2 of John's Gospel. At Passover, Jesus went to Jerusalem, to the temple and, finding it desecrated by moneychangers and merchants, He "drove them out of the temple,

5—C.P.

and the sheep, and the oxen; and poured out the changers' money, and overthrew the tables" (John 2:15). After that incident, "many believed in his name, when they saw the miracles which he did. But Jesus did not commit himself unto them, because he knew all men, and needed not that any should testify of man: *for he knew what was in man*" (John 2:23-25, emphasis supplied).

Though "many believed in his name," Jesus wouldn't commit Himself to them, because belief in His name, in and of itself, wasn't enough to change what was in them—and what was in them wasn't good.

"There is no one righteous, not even one; there is no one who understands, no one who seeks God. All have turned away, they have together become worthless; there is no one who does good, not even one."

"Their throats are open graves; their tongues practice deceit."

"The poison of vipers is on their lips."

"Their mouths are full of cursing and bitterness."

"Their feet are swift to shed blood; ruin and misery mark their ways, and the way of peace they do not know."

"There is no fear of God before their eyes" (Romans 3:10-18, NIV).

Clifford Goldstein

Paul wrote these words almost two millennia ago, quoting something written five centuries before. Obviously, even after 2,500 years, we haven't changed; in fact, most would agree, we're worse.

No doubt, everyone is capable of some goodness, but that doesn't make them "good," any more than staying off the bottle for two days makes an alcoholic a teetotaler. In *The House of the Dead*, Feodor Dostoyevsky wrote about crude, hardened prisoners, everyone from mass rapists to parricides, who even in the harsh, painful circumstances of a Siberian prison camp were at times capable of selfless and random acts of love and kindness. Yet who would call these men "good"?

A liberal professor at Harvard told her students that the Christian doctrine of man's inherent sinfulness was irrefutable. All you have to do, she said, was to look out the window—the effects were everywhere. For an even better perspective, though, her students should have looked, not into a glass that lets light pass through, but into one that reflects it back into their faces.

Interestingly enough, too, belief in Jesus, in and of itself, wouldn't have changed what they would see. After John C. Salvi III, who believed in Jesus, was jailed for murdering two abortion-clinic receptionists, a Virginia Protestant minister, who also believed in Jesus, stood outside the jail and shouted into a megaphone, "Thank you for what you did in the name of Jesus!"

Susan Smith—a church-going, praying, believer in Jesus—strapped her two infants in the seat of her car, rolled the car into a lake, and drowned them.

"Come what may," said a professing Christian, "I shall always love God, shall pray to Him, shall remain faithful to the Catholic Church, and shall defend it even if I should be expelled from it."

Who was this lover of God and defender of the faith? Heinrich Himmler.

No wonder Jesus said. "Ye must be born again."

17

In the six verses (John 3:3-8) in which Jesus stressed the new birth three times, He twice linked it to "the kingdom of God." Though debate exists over what the "kingdom of God" means, ultimately it must refer to the eschatological kingdom that God ushers in at the end of the age.

"There was given him dominion, and glory, and a kingdom, that all people, nations, and languages, should serve him: his dominion is an everlasting dominion, which shall not pass away, and his kingdom that which shall not be destroyed" (Daniel 7:14).

God's kingdom isn't a remake of the world's. The Lord won't just patch, plug, and paint over what's here. Things are too far gone for that. The earth needs more than a remodeling. Everything, from the ground up, will be demolished and redone.

"Behold, I make all things new" (Revelation 21:5). "For behold, I create new heavens and a new earth" (Isaiah 65:17). "And I saw a new heaven and a new earth: for the first heaven and the first earth were passed away" (Revelation 21:1).

"Looking for and hasting unto the coming of the day of God, wherein the heavens being on fire shall be dissolved, and the elements shall melt with fervent heat? Nevertheless we, according to his promise, look for new heavens and a new earth, wherein dwelleth righteousness" (2 Peter 3:12, 13).

But why does Jesus link God's kingdom—i.e., the new heavens and the new earth—to the new birth? The answer's obvious: because the Lord is working through the new birth to prepare us, even now, to live in the new heaven and the new earth. The cosmic renewal has already begun—not with the rocks, the trees, or the sky, but with us, when we're "born again."

"Therefore, if any man be in Christ, he is a new creature; old things are passed away; behold, all things are become new" (2 Corinthians 5:17).

God will, eventually, give us new bodies on a new earth; until then, He's remaking only one part of all creation, an important part in fact, and that is—our hearts. Everything else will just have to wait.

Clifford Goldstein

"The new birth is the prerequisite," wrote evangelical scholar Michael Williams, "it is the entrance requirement of the kingdom of God, and it is for everyone. . . . Every person, by virtue of being human, is a sinner and is in need of the transforming power, the revivification and redirection of the new birth. Only then will they be fit citizens for the kingdom of God."

"Create in me a clean heart, O God; and renew a right spirit within me" (Psalm 51:10). "A new heart also will I give you, and a new spirit will I put within you: and I will take away the stony heart out of your flesh, and I will give you an heart of flesh" (Ezekiel 36:26).

Through the new birth, God prepares us for when all things will, in a sense, be "born" or created anew. We're getting a head start, probably because we so desperately need one.

"The creation waits in eager expectation for the sons of God to be revealed. For the creation was subjected to frustration, not by its own choice, but by the will of the one who subjected it, in hope that the creation itself will be liberated from its bondage to decay and brought into the glorious freedom of the children of God. We know that the whole creation has been groaning as in the pains of childbirth right up to the present time. Not

Children of the Promise

only so, but we ourselves, who have the first - fruits of the Spirit, groan inwardly as we wait eagerly for our adoption as sons, the redemption of our bodies" (Romans 8:19-23, NIV).

Paul is talking here about the ultimate salvation of mankind, the ultimate erasure of sin and its consequences throughout "the whole creation." And one small, but important, aspect of that operation is when we, who await "the redemption of our bodies," are, in the meantime, changed in our hearts—a process that begins with the new birth.

18

More than 2,500 years ago, the Greek philosopher Heraclitus wrote that "you can't step into the same river twice," meaning that just as the river constantly changes, just as new, different water flows in every part so that it's not the same river the second time you step in—everything else in the world changes as well.

His student, Cratylus, meanwhile, argued that you can't "even step in the same river once," because the mere act of stepping into the water changes the river, so that you really can't step into the same river at all.

Whether you agree with either Heraclitus or Cratylus, a fundamental aspect of all physical reality is change. From the position of the stars in the expanding universe to the molecular formation of matter, everything, everywhere, constantly changes. Nothing is the same now as it was a moment ago, nor will it be the same a moment later.

"All things," wrote Heraclitus, "are in flux."

Ourselves included. From conception to carnal dissolution, we undergo incessant, irreversible transformations. Whether sleeping or speaking, healing or hurting, growing or shrinking, gorging or fasting, swimming or sitting—whatever we do, however, wherever, and whenever we do it, we constantly change—physically and mentally converting from one state to another.

French philosopher Herni Bergson wrote:

> A slight effort of attention, would reveal to me that there is no feeling, no idea, no volition which is not undergoing change every moment. . . . My memory is there, which conveys something of the past into the present. My mental state, as it advances on the road of time, is continually swelling with the duration that it accumulates; it goes on increasing— rolling upon itself, as a snowball in the snow. . . . Our personality, which is being built up each instant with its accumulated experiences, changes without stopping. . . . Thus our personality shoots, grows, and ripens without

Clifford Goldstein

ceasing. Each of its moments is something new added to what was before.

Whether the sun converting hydrogen into heat and light, or cells in plants and animals converting air, food, and water into energy—conversion is the essence of change. The ancient Greeks believed, incredibly enough, that matter never disappears, it just converts to something else, a principle expressed thousands of years later as a fundamental law of thermodynamics: "Matter is neither created or destroyed, just changed [or converted] from one form to another."

But change, the conversion of matter from one form to another, doesn't always have to be good. In fact, another law of thermodynamics states that things, left to themselves, tend toward entropy, toward disorganization and confusion. In the same way that the planets, in and of themselves, won't automatically revolve around the sun in ellipses, few things automatically change for the good unless acted upon at some point (often at their creation) by an outside source.

This principle holds especially true for the human mind, which is incessantly molded by a barrage of information. That's why the new birth—which includes a radical conversion of the mind—is so important.

"Verily I say unto you, Except ye be converted, and

Children of the Promise

become as little children, ye shall not enter into the kingdom of heaven" (Matthew 18:3).

Yet this change doesn't come naturally. We no more have an innate bent toward goodness than do the planets toward revolving around the sun. Nothing in our genes inheres towards conversion; in fact, it's because of our genes that the change must come from outside of us. If left alone, we would—like everything else—tend toward entropy. Thus, we must have an external source to work in us—and that source is the Holy Spirit, the agent in the new-birth experience.

> Except a man be born of water and of the Spirit, he cannot enter into the kingdom of God. That which is born of the flesh is flesh; and that which is born of the Spirit is spirit. Marvel not that I say unto thee, Ye must be born again. The wind bloweth where it listeth, and thou hearest the sound thereof, but canst not tell whence it cometh, and whither it goeth: so is every one that is born of the Spirit (John 3:5-8).

The essence of our nature is change. Whether that change will be for good or evil, for God or the world, depends upon one factor: whether we have been born of the Spirit.

19

When Christ said that we must be born again, He was talking spiritually, not literally. Whatever the incidental physical changes (one missionary tells of a Japanese actor who, after his conversion, could no longer play the role of a villain, so dramatically had his face altered), the new birth is, essentially, a phenomenon of mind, not flesh. To the extent that a radical reordering of attitude, thought, emotion, and motive affects flesh, the new birth does have physical repercussions, but at the core it's a matter of mind, not matter.

"He came unto his own, and his own received him not. But as many as received him, to them gave he power to become the sons of God, even to them that believe on his name: Which were born, not of blood, nor of the will of the flesh, nor of the will of man, but of God" (John 1:11-13).

"Beloved, let us love one another: for love is of God; and every one that loveth is born of God" (1 John 4:7).

"Whosoever believeth that Jesus is the Christ is born of God" (1 John 5:1).

To be born of God is the same as being born again: it's the spiritual rebirth that happens only through the Holy Spirit: "Marvel not that I said unto thee, Ye must be born again. The wind bloweth where it listeth, and thou hearest the sound thereof, but canst not tell whence it cometh, and whither it goeth: so is every one that is born of the Spirit" (John 3:7, 8).

Before His ascension, Jesus promised that the Holy Spirit would come in His place, and through Him people would be convicted of truth:

Nevertheless I tell you the truth; it is expedient for you that I go away: for if I go not away, the Comforter will not come unto you; but if I depart, I will send him unto you. And when he is come, he will reprove the world of sin, and of righteousness, and of judgment. . . . Howbeit when he, the Spirit of truth, is come, he will guide you into all truth (John 16:7, 8, 13).

Clifford Goldstein

The new birth, which helps bring us into conformity with "all truth," is ultimately the work of the Comforter. Without Him, we could no more be "born in the Spirit" than we could, without our mother, be born in the flesh.

> But when the kindness and generosity of God our Saviour dawned upon the world, then, not for any good deeds of our own, but because he was merciful, he saved us through the water of rebirth and the renewing power of the Holy Spirit. For he sent down the Spirit upon us plentifully through Jesus Christ our Saviour, so that, justified by his grace, we might in hope become heirs to eternal life" (Titus 3:4-7, NEB).

Because of His mercy and love, God justified us in Jesus Christ, and through Jesus Christ He sends the Spirit, and through the work of the Holy Spirit we're born again.

John wrote, too, that Jesus "was the true Light, which lighteth every man that cometh into the world" (John 1:9), an illumination that comes through the Holy Spirit, His Representative on earth. Yet, even if "every man" is influenced by the Spirit—many, if not most, are never born again.

Why?

Children of the Promise

The answer can be found by looking at some new-birth experiences, because by understanding what has happened to those who have them, we can understand what happens to those who don't.

20

Probably the most dramatic born-again experience ever recorded occurred almost two thousand years ago, when Saul of Tarsus became the apostle Paul. In Acts 22, Paul recounts—before a mob thirsting for his blood—what happened.

As I made my journey, and was come nigh unto Damascus about noon, suddenly there shone from heaven a great light round about me. And I fell unto the ground, and heard a voice saying unto me, "Saul, Saul, why persecutest thou me?" And I answered, "Who art thou, Lord?" And he said unto me, "I am Jesus of Nazareth, whom thou persecutest."

6—C.P.

Children of the Promise

> And they that were with me saw indeed the
> light, and were afraid; but they heard not the
> voice of him that spake to me. And I said,
> "What shall I do, Lord?" (Acts 22:6-10).

Interestingly enough, Damascus road wasn't the
first place that Saul felt convicted about Jesus Christ.
Ellen White wrote, "Saul had taken a prominent part
in the trial and conviction of Stephen, and the striking evidences of God's presence with the martyr had
led Saul to doubt the righteousness of the cause he
had espoused against the followers of Jesus. His mind
was deeply stirred." (*The Acts of the Apostles*, 112, 113).

Saul was eventually convinced by the religious
leaders that Christ was a false messiah, though "not
without severe trial did Saul come to his conclusion. . . . And having fully decided that the priests were
right, Saul became very bitter in his opposition to the
doctrines taught by the disciples of Jesus" (ibid., 113).

Nevertheless, everything changed on the road to
Damascus. Just a few moments earlier, Saul determined to arrest the followers of Jesus; now he falls to
the ground and becomes one of those followers, cry-
ing out, "What shall I do, Lord?"

This is the new birth. Not everyone will have such
a dramatic, sudden conversion. But even if they don't
drop to the ground before a blinding light, sooner or
later, in one manner or another—often (but not al-

Clifford Goldstein

ways) from the gentle, continuous promptings of the still small voice—everyone must completely surrender to God, just as Saul did on the Damascus road.

Otherwise, they'll never be born again.

21

Another new birth, not as dramatic as Saul's (and hardly as consequential) is worth depicting, but only because I know it so well.

In my early twenties, my existence had become subservient to only one thing—writing fiction. Consumed by this irrepressible passion to create art out of words, I had spent more than two years working on a novel and fully expected to spend at least two years more before completing it.

Everything was relative to the book. Anything I did, and however long I did it; wherever I went, and however long I stayed—was determined by the impact on my writing. In that sense, the book controlled my life outside of it as much, if not more, than I controlled the lives within it.

Then one evening, as I put my fingers on the typewriter keys, Jesus Christ—through a powerful manifestation of the Holy Spirit—came to me in my room and said, *Cliff, you have been playing with Me long enough. If you want Me tonight, burn the book!*

Now, this experience didn't just happen in a vacuum. Over the previous few years, I had had some spiritual awakenings, to the point that I not only believed in God, but could even accept the reality of Christianity (which for a Jew is hard stuff). Yet whatever the spiritual longings that stirred within, including the care and feeding of my soul—it all came a distant second to the book, which was the only god I worshiped.

But now I was confronted by the God who had created me and by His overwhelming claims upon me. I couldn't serve both God and the book. It was either my god or God Himself. For hours I pled, cajoled, argued, rationalized, and even at one point fled, but the Holy Spirit was dogged: If I wanted the Lord, I must burn the book.

So I burned it—an outward manifestation of my inward desire to go all the way with Christ, whatever the cost. Like Saul on the road to Damascus, I had surrendered, unconditionally. And that night, wrapped in the smoke of all that I had once been, I was born again.

22

Just sentenced to five years, a criminal stood before the judge and exclaimed, "But your honor, all the factors of my life, even from before I was born, drove me to what I did. Everything—my upbringing, heredity, and environment—caused me to commit that robbery. I had no choice. How can you send me to prison?"

"Because," replied the judge, looming from his bench, "all the factors of *my* life, even from before I was born—including my upbringing, hereditary, and environment—cause me to sentence you to prison. I, too, have no choice."

For centuries, humans have struggled with questions about free will, determinism, and fate. In his

Clifford Goldstein

play, *Oedipus the King*, written 2,500 years ago, Sophocles wrote about King Laius and Queen Jocasta, who hear a prophesy that their infant son will grow up to murder his father and marry his mother. In response, they do everything they can—even ordering the infant to be left on a mountaintop to die—so that the prophesy won't come to pass. And, yet, in the final scene, Oedipus kills Laius and marries Jocasta, just as predicted.

American philosopher, Richard Taylor, in his *Metaphysics*, wrote that "it is not hard to suppose, as we have seen, that everything that happens is wholly determined by what went before it, and hence that whatever happens at any future time is the only thing that can then happen, given what precedes it."

Even from a Christian perspective, free will and determinism aren't easily resolved. Suppose Pilate had decided, as he almost did, to let Christ go? Would the plan of salvation have been scrapped? Did the outcome of the great controversy between Christ and Satan, and all the issues involved, depend upon the bad choice of a weak and vacillating governor? If not, how can Pilate be condemned for a choice that he was fated, or predetermined, to make?

As Adventists, we accept free will on faith, just as we do righteousness through Christ as our substitutionary atonement, because however difficult the questions associated with free will may be, they're

Children of the Promise

easier than these: *Could a loving God send people to hell who had no choice in the decisions they made? If some are predestined to be lost, no matter their choices, then doesn't the Lord become capricious, arbitrary, and a respecter of persons? How could God be "not willing that any should perish, but that all should come to repentance" (2 Peter 3:9) and yet predetermine beforehand who repents and who perishes?*

Somehow, we don't know how, God knows the beginning from the end, can bring prophecy to pass, and can accomplish His purposes in the earth, despite the free will bestowed upon us and the choices that free will allows us to make.

In every person, a type of "neutral zone" exists, an inviolable region where we exercise autonomy. We each have our own "sacred space" in which we rule, and where even God Himself won't enter unless invited. This is where our choices, for good or bad, are made. And it is in this zone where we, using our free will, respond to the prompting of the Holy Spirit.

"In the matchless gift of His Son," wrote Ellen White, "God has encircled the whole world with an atmosphere of grace as real as the air which circulates around the globe. All who *choose* to breathe this life-giving atmosphere will live and grow up to the stature of men and women in Christ Jesus" (*Steps to Christ*, 68, emphasis supplied).

Questions about who has or hasn't had a new-birth

Clifford Goldstein

experience boil down to our reaction to the Holy Spirit. We can't make ourselves be born again, but we can *choose* to allow the Holy Spirit to do that work in us. Whatever the circumstances of our life, whatever providence, chance, or choice throw our way now, only one of two ultimate destinies—eternal life or eternal death—awaits us. Which one depends upon whether we, using our free will, choose to be born again.

23

"When Christ calls a man," wrote Dietrich Bonhoeffer, "he bids him come and die."

Bonhoeffer, understood better than most, the meaning of those words. When German Protestants were almost universally hailing the virtues of Nazism (or at least not bemoaning its evils), this gifted theologian and preacher opposed the regime. As Hitler instituted laws against the Jews, Bonhoeffer immediately, and openly, argued that Christians had an obligation to "jam a spoke in the wheel of the state" when it oppressed innocent people. Dangerous words when the state wheel was being turned by Adolph Hitler and Heinrich Himmler.

Bonhoeffer had visited the United States and, at one

point, almost stayed. However, believing that it was his Christian duty to work for the defeat of the Nazis, he sailed back into the arms of his black-shirt enemies.

"I must live through this difficult period of our national history with the Christian people of Germany," he wrote. "I will have no right to participate in the reconstruction of Christian life in Germany after the war if I do not share the trials of this time with my people."

Eventually, Bonhoeffer was arrested by the Gestapo for his anti-Nazi activity. Two years and four days later, the Nazis hung him just outside of Berlin.

"When Christ calls a man, he bids him come and die."

Unlike Bonhoeffer, most Christians don't end up as martyrs. Yet there is a death that all must "die" if they will ever be "born again."

In the physical world, life always precedes death. Death implies life, because only that which is alive can die. Life, then, is the necessary precursor to death.

In the Christian realm, however, the order is reversed.

"For ye are *dead*, and your *life* is hid with Christ in God" (Colossians 3:3, emphasis supplied).

Notice, the order is death, then life.

"Now if we be *dead* with Christ, we believe that we shall also *live* with him" (Romans 6:8, emphasis supplied).

Children of the Promise

Again, the order is death, then life.

"Therefore we are buried with him by baptism into *death*: that like as Christ was raised up from the dead by the glory of the Father, even so we should walk in newness of *life*" (Romans 6:4, emphasis supplied).

Death, then life.

"It is a faithful saying: For it we be *dead* with him, we shall also *live* with him" (2 Timothy 2:11, emphasis supplied).

"For I through the law am *dead* to the law, that I might *live* unto God" (Galatians 2:19, emphasis supplied).

"And you, who were *dead* in trespasses and the uncircumcision of your flesh, God made *alive* together with him, having forgiven us all our trespasses" (Colossians 2:13, RSV, emphasis supplied).

"Always carrying in the body the *death* of Jesus, so that the *life* of Jesus may also be manifested in our bodies" (2 Corinthians 4:10, RSV, emphasis supplied).

Whatever their immediate context, these verses say that we must die in order to live in Christ. As Jesus said: "For whoever will save his life shall lose it: but whosoever will lose his life for my sake, the same shall save it" (Luke 9:24).

In the natural word, we're born and then we die; in the spiritual realm, we die, and then we're born again.

24

Central to many spiritual belief systems is that mysterious, hard-to-define entity known as self.

Eastern and New Age philosophy stress that "the self is God—realize it."

A guru teaches that self is nothing, that we are, in essence, nothing, and that the key to spiritual fulfillment is experiencing your own nothingness.

Years after dying at the foot of his toilet, jammies at his feet, "Elvis" appears to a woman and says that she needs to get in touch with her real self.

In contrast, Christianity teaches that the only way to deal with self is—not to realize it, not to imagine that it doesn't exist, and not to get in touch with it—but to *die to it*. Self, in and of itself, isn't the answer;

it's the problem. Self shouldn't be cultivated, watered, or nurtured—it should be crucified.

"I am crucified with Christ: nevertheless I live; yet not I, but Christ liveth in me: and the life which I now live in the flesh I live by the faith of the Son of God, who loved me, and gave himself for me" (Galatians 2:20).

What does it mean to die in order to have life? To be crucified with Christ in order to be born again? The answer is found in Saul's experience on the road to Damascus where he was born again. All that he had lived for, all that was the essence of his identity as a Pharisee, a defender of the traditions, a leader of the Jews—all this, Saul died to. He had surrendered His will, His life, to Jesus Christ, and this surrender is a crucial component of the new-birth experience.

Saul's life (in contrast to Paul's) was a microcosm of the human condition *prior* to conversion. Those who haven't surrendered to Christ, who haven't yielded to the wooing of His Spirit are, like Saul, battling Christ whether they know it or not (and you don't have to be persecuting Christ's followers to be battling Him, either). "He that is not with me," Jesus said, "is against me" (Matthew 12:30).

In whatever way the Holy Spirit moves upon us—whether by a settling into truth, intellectually and experientially, or a dramatic, instant conversion or something unique in between—it's not how you die that counts, but simply that you do.

But you can't kill yourself, not in this context, any more than you can hang yourself on a cross. You'll hammer in maybe only one nail at best, and that might make you suffer, but it won't kill you. God alone can bring about your death to self, but He won't unless you let Him. This isn't murder, it's mercy killing, assisted suicide, but only after you make a conscious choice to die to your miserable, guilt-ridden, sin-sick self and live for Jesus Christ instead.

"Therefore we are buried with him by baptism into death: that like as Christ was raised up from the dead by the glory of the Father, even so we also should walk in newness of life" (Romans 6:4).

Decades ago, half-drunk and miserable in the back of his chauffeur-driven limousine, Coca-Cola magnate Asa Chandler Jr. was suddenly convicted by the Holy Spirit. That night, in the back of his limo, he chose to die to himself and live for Jesus.

"The central thing in Christianity," he later testified, "is the final and total yielding of the self, its renunciation and rejection and the entire surrender of the life to the will and way of God."

No matter how well you know the Bible, how much theology you understand, how kind, loving, and giving you are, to have a new-birth experience, you must by faith surrender your dreams, hopes, plans, and goals—in essence, the totality of your life—to God.

Children of the Promise

This is the death Christ meant when He said, "For whosoever will save his life shall lose it: but whosoever will lose his life for my sake, the same shall save it" (Luke 9:24). It is also the death that you must die if you are to be "born again."

25

In my earliest days as a believer, when I tried to convert anything, whether or not it breathed, I took a homeless person to an Italian restaurant. His name was Bud, and his dirty shadow had been lurking along the streets of Gainesville, Florida, for years. Tall, lanky, with a boyish, mischievous grin, he looked like an adult Dennis the Menace with AIDS. He had been without a bath as long as he had been without a shave.

As I tried to get him to surrender to Christ, to make a commitment, he resisted my words, syllable by syllable. Understanding the death to self that conversion required, I looked at this scant outline of a man—homeless, filthy, unemployed, unemployable!—and I couldn't fathom what it was he wouldn't give up.

Children of the Promise

With incredulity I asked, "Man, what in the world are you holding on to?"

He never answered. He was too busy sucking ketchup out of the red plastic bottle that sat on the table next to the salt and pepper.

That question could be asked of anyone, whether they live on the street or parade down it in a gold Cadillac. Whether you're drowning in a bottle of Seagram's, or you own Seagram's, in the end, in the face of eternity, the only question that remains is, "Man, what in the world are you holding on to?" Or, as Jesus put it, "For what is a man profited, if he shall gain the whole world, and lose his own soul?" (Matthew 16:26).

There's no option, alternative, or escape; to be born again, you must die to self.

Now death, particularly to self, isn't pleasant, at least at first, which is why people always resist. Our sinful, egocentric nature clings to self—pampers, nurtures, and protects it. Yet whatever the seasonal pleasures, living for self just doesn't work, not in the long run. We were created to live for God; yet, because of the Fall, we live for self instead, and by constantly feeding self, we feed the source of our sorrows. The most greedy, avaricious, and rapacious souls are usually the unhappiest; and the more they coddle their avarice, the unhappier they become. It's the nature of fallen self never to be satisfied. Self can never have enough, for the mere act of feeding it only increases its appetite for more.

"Then I looked on all the works that my hands had wrought," said the wealthiest man of antiquity, "and on the labour that I had laboured to do: and, behold, all was vanity and vexation of spirit, and there was no profit under the sun" (Ecclesiastes 2:11).

That's why the greatest thing that can happen to a soul is to be dead to self and alive to God. However painful that death, at least initially, it is what Martin Luther called "the joyful exchange," in which you change an egocentric, insatiable self for one centered on God, the only One who can satisfy you.

"You are to *give* all,–" wrote Ellen White, "your heart, your will, your service,–give yourself to Him to obey all His requirements; and you must *take* all,– Christ, the fullness of all blessing, to abide in your heart, to be your strength, your righteousness, your everlasting helper,–to give you power to obey" (*Steps to Christ*, 70, emphasis supplied).

This total giving of self and total taking of Christ is *the* transition, the "crossing over" (from which possibly the word *Hebrew* originates), the passage from flesh to the Spirit, from bondage to freedom, and from death to life.

"Having predestined us unto the adoption of children by Jesus Christ to himself, according to the good pleasure of his will, to the praise of the glory of his grace, wherein he hath made us accepted in the beloved. In whom we have redemption through his blood, the forgiveness of sins, according to the riches of his grace" (Ephesians 1:5-7).

The riches of this grace include the freedom, power, and peace that come to those who, having already died with Christ ("For ye are dead"), are now alive to God through Him ("and your life is hid with God in Jesus Christ"—Colossians 3:3).

These are the same ones who—being "found in him, not having . . . [their] own righteousness, which is of the law, but that which is through the faith of Christ, the righteousness which is of God by faith" (Philippians 3:9)—partake of the assurance, the peace, and promises that Christ gives to those who, by faith, choose to partake of His righteousness.

These are those who "have put on the new man, which is renewed in knowledge, after the image of him that created him" (Colossians 3:10), and thus who enjoy the fruits thereof.

26

"Two souls, alas, are lodged within my breast," wrote Goethe, "which struggle there for undivided reign."

Two forces do struggle for undivided reign within us—self (prompted by its indefatigable encourager, supporter, and cheerleader, the devil) and Jesus Christ, manifested through the Holy Spirit. We, alone, have been given the choice of whom, ultimately, wins. When we choose to die to self through faith, Satan loses his supreme grip, and Christ, as a personal force living within us, becomes the overriding reality of our lives.

Only those who have experienced it themselves can know what a joy it is to partake of the living Christ, to have His Spirit dwell within as He nurtures, heals, guides, renews, comforts, rebukes, and purifies. Almost two thousand years ago, Jesus promised, "Lo, I am with you alway, even unto the end of the world" (Matthew 28:20), and through the new birth, we experience the reality of His presence with us in an intimate, dynamic, and personal way.

"A few years ago," said singer Johnny Cash, "I was hooked on drugs. I dreaded to wake up in the morning. There was no joy, peace, or happiness in my life. Then one day, in my helplessness, I turned my life completely over to God. Now I can't wait to get up in the morning to study my Bible. Sometimes the words out of the Scriptures leap into my heart. This does not mean that all my problems are solved, or that I have reached any state of perfection. However, my life has been turned around. I have been born again!"

The new birth is the means by which Christianity is realized in the life of the believer. It's the difference between reading about love and being in love. It's when Jesus becomes the center of our life, not just our theology. Doctrines, beliefs, dogma, and creeds—even true ones—don't make you a Christian any more than reading about flight makes you a bird. The only kind of Christianity that justifies, sanctifies, and ultimately glorifies is one that becomes a personal experience in the heart of a soul, the kind that results from the new birth. What turned Saul into Paul wasn't a theological discussion on clean and unclean meats; it was the reality of Jesus Christ in His life.

"Always bearing about in the body the dying of the Lord Jesus," Paul wrote, "that the life also of Jesus might be made manifest in our body. For we which live are alway delivered unto death for Jesus' sake, that the life also of Jesus might be made manifest in our mortal flesh" (2 Corinthians 4:10, 11).

Paul promised that the "fruit of the Spirit is love, joy, peace, longsuffering, gentleness, goodness, faith, meekness, temperance" (Galatians 5:22), and this fruit is made manifest in us, not because we assent to certain biblical truths, but because we have been "born again."

Jesus said, "Behold, I stand at the door, and knock: if any man hear my voice, and open the door, I will come in to him, and will sup with him, and he with me" (Revelation 3:20), and the new birth entails this opening of the door so that Christ can, indeed, come in and "sup" with us.

Peter wrote, "Whereby are given unto us exceeding great and precious promises: that by these ye might be partakers of the divine nature" (2 Peter 1:4), and the new birth leads to the reality of having these "exceeding great and precious promises" fulfilled in our lives.

John proclaimed, "for this is the love of God, that we keep His commandments" (1 John 5:3), and the only way we can keep them is through the power of Christ dwelling in us, which begins with the new birth. "For whatsoever is born of God overcometh the world: and this is the victory that overcometh the world, even our faith" (1 John 5:4). Thus, being "born of God" begins the process of living by faith, which gives us the victory over the things of the world.

Of course, being born again isn't an immediate cure-all. All your problems don't abruptly vanish, all your sins don't instantly go away, all your pains don't suddenly stop, and all your relationships aren't healed the moment you're born again.

Instead, through the new birth you're now in a new relationship with God, one in which you've surrendered your life and will to Him so that He's able to work in you "according to his own purpose and grace" (2 Timothy 1:9). This involves a daily, continuous process of healing, nurturing, and sanctifying that ultimately makes you a new person in Jesus Christ.

In short, the new birth is the means by which God's promise that "he which hath begun a good work in you will perform it until the day of Jesus Christ" (Philippians 1:6) first becomes real in the life of a sinner redeemed, pardoned, and justified by the blood of the Lamb.

27

In the late 1970s, while living on a kibbutz beside the Sea of Galilee, I roomed with a big Belgian who had left home because he had been involved in a bank robbery. One sticky summer night, drunk, he smashed our room to pieces and was kicked off the kibbutz the next morning. Before leaving, he looked me in the eyes and uttered, "*I wahnt a nu lif.*"

How many millions, having made a mess of their *lif*, desperately want a new one. Yet no matter what they try—even moving to a new city, starting a new job, getting a new spouse, whatever—their new lives usually aren't much better than their old ones because, however much they change the externals, the internal remains the same, and so nothing really changes at all.

In contrast, the Bible promises a new life in Christ. Jesus might not give us a new home, a better-paying job, a more-agreeable spouse, because these are only externals. Instead, Christ gives us a new heart, which alone leads to a new existence.

"I will sprinkle clean water upon you and ye shall be clean. . . . A new heart also will I give you, and a new spirit will I put within you" (Ezekiel 36: 25, 26).

"Create in me a clean heart, O God, and renew a right spirit within me" (Psalm 51:10).

"For he is not a Jew, which is one outwardly; neither is that circumcision, which is outward in the flesh: But he is a Jew, which is one inwardly; and circumcision is that of the heart, in the spirit, and not in the letter" (Romans 2:28, 29).

Though the circumstances vary from person to person, the principle is the same: the Holy Spirit moves upon us, and we respond by dying to self, a total surrender of our will to God's. We are, then, born again, and instead of living in the flesh, alienated and separated from the Lord, we now live in the Spirit (the same Spirit that raised Christ from the dead!) under the gentle guiding hand of God. What happens from there is the "newness of life" (Romans 6:4) in Christ Jesus that Paul wrote about.

"Therefore, if anyone is in Christ, he is a new creation; the old has passed away, behold the new has come" (2 Corinthians 5:17, RSV).

This new life is an ongoing, dynamic process in which God cleanses, heals, sanctifies, and transforms those who have surrendered to Christ, in order to make them into His moral image. "Lie not one to another, seeing that you have put off the old man with his deeds: And have put on the new man, which is renewed in knowledge after the image of him that created him" (Colossians 3: 9, 10).

We aren't given just a new status, but a new state as well. However much the new birth is based on justification alone, it never ends there, because justification isn't an end, but a means to an end, and that end is the total restoration of humanity to what it was before the Fall.

"Just as we have borne the image of the man of dust, we shall also bear the image of the man of heaven.... Lo! I tell you a mystery. We shall not all sleep, but we shall all be changed, in a moment, in the twinkling of an eye, at the last trumpet. For the trumpet will sound, and the dead will be raised imperishable, and we shall be changed" (1 Corinthians 15:49, 51-52, RSV).

Though that final restoration happens only after we are given new bodies, the new birth is the decisive, crucial phase in the process. "You must be born again," because the new birth leads to a new life, and a new life entails our slow, but promised, moral transformation, a regeneration from a life enslaved to the flesh to one free in the Spirit, from a life of emptiness and alienation to one of fullness and joy in fellowship with God the Father and His Son Jesus Christ.

This new birth and new life are something that no science, psychology, philosophy, or even theology can make real. Parents can give a lot to their children, but not this. You can't inherit a new life in Christ any more than you can inherit fluency in French.

"But as many as received him, to them gave he power to become the sons of God, even to them that believe on his name: which were born, not of blood, nor of the will of the flesh nor of the will of man, but of God" (John 1:12, 13).

Other than our conscious choice to receive and then abide in Him, the process is God's alone. That's why a life in the Spirit results only from our individual surrender to God. It is a supernatural experience, and only one who has this experience knows what it means to be born of God, and then to live a new life in Christ, where he walks "not after the flesh but after the Spirit" (Romans 8:1).

28

After the new birth, sinful flesh remains all around us. In fact, it still clings to our bones. Being born again doesn't guarantee absolute freedom from the suffering, hardship, disappointment, and the failures due to sin, either. It just changes the rules of the game.

And the first rule is our complete dependence upon God. "Without me," Jesus said, "ye can do nothing" (John 15:5), especially without Him we cannot enjoy the abundance of life God promises to those who love and obey Him.

This truth shouldn't be that hard to learn (though often is), because the mere act of surrendering to the Lord indicates a dependence on Him. The more you give of yourself to God, the more you must then depend upon Him; a total surrender means total dependence.

This dependance doesn't end with justification, either. Ellen White wrote that many "have trusted in Christ for the forgiveness of sin, but now they seek by their own efforts to live aright. But every such effort must fail. . . . Our growth in grace, our joy, our usefulness,—all depend upon our union with Christ" (*Steps to Christ*, 69).

However, just as with the new birth, we have a crucial role to play in living this new life in Christ. "As ye have therefore received Christ Jesus the Lord, so walk ye in him" (Colossians 2:6). We received Christ by surrendering ourselves to Him. That's not only how we're born again, but how we abide in Him as well—through a continuous, daily surrender of our will to His.

After having burned the book I had been writing for two years, I have often prayed, *Lord, I wish I had a book to burn every day!*—not as any attempt to earn merit, but as a visible manifestation of my conscious choice to live only for God, not for self.

Life in Christ, then, is a melding of the human and the divine; whatever the supernatural manifestations of the Spirit, we have the crucial, volitional role of yielding to His promptings and the commands of the Word. True surrender to God always involves action. We obey the one to whom we yield.

Clifford Goldstein

After being born of the Spirit, we have a relationship with God in which He can now touch the inner sanctum of our soul. Through prayer, fellowship, and the reading of His Word, we have opened the door to Jesus Christ.

Next, through communion with God, we better understand right from wrong, good from evil, truth from error—not from a subjective human perspective, but from God's divine one. By concentrating upon Christ's love, the beauty and perfection of His character, His self-denial, His purity, and His holiness as revealed in His Word, we learn about what God wants us to be.

Then, through the prompting of our conscience by the Holy Spirit, we are impressed to act upon this knowledge. When we are faced with trials, temptations, and the carnal cries of the flesh, the Holy Spirit impresses us with what God would have us to do. The image of Christ is before us, to emulate and follow.

Finally, if we choose what the Bible and the Holy Spirit tell us is right, we have been promised divine power to act upon that choice. "There hath no temptation taken you but such as is common to man; but God is faithful, who will not suffer you to be tempted above that you are able; but will with the temptation make a way of escape, that ye may be able to bear it" (1 Corinthians 10:13).

The weak link, of course, is ourselves, because

whatever God's promises, even born-again Seventh-day Adventists don't always avail themselves of them. The Spirit touches the conscience but never forces the will.

That's why, fundamental to a new life in Christ, must be the constant realization that our standing with God depends upon the merits of Christ, separate and distinct from ourselves. We must always keep before us that, as High Priest in the heavenly sanctuary, Jesus applies His merits in our behalf—especially when we fall (because that's when we need them the most)!

"My little children, these things write I unto you, that ye sin not. And if any man sin, we have an advocate with the Father, Jesus Christ the righteous" (1 John 2:1). "Wherefore he is able also to save them to the uttermost that come unto God by him, seeing he ever liveth to make intercession for them" (Hebrews 7:25).

In a chapter titled, "Joshua and the Angel," Ellen White depicts Christ as our Intercessor and Advocate:

> The high priest cannot defend himself or his people from Satan's accusations. He does not claim that Israel are free from fault. In his filthy garments, symbolizing the sins of the people, which he bears as their representative, he stands before the Angel, confessing their guilt,

Clifford Goldstein

yet pointing to their repentance and humiliation, relying upon the mercy of a sin-pardoning Redeemer and in faith claiming the promises of God. . . . Man cannot meet these charges himself. In his sin-stained garments, confessing his guilt, he stands before God. But Jesus our Advocate presents an effectual plea in behalf of all who by repentance and faith have committed the keeping of their souls to Him. He pleads their cause and vanquishes their accuser by the mighty arguments of Calvary. His perfect obedience to God's law, even unto the death of the cross, has given Him all power in heaven and in earth, and He claims of His Father mercy and reconciliation for guilty man" (*Testimonies for the Church*, 5: 468, 471).

The great hope for those born again is that while God molds them into His image, they have already been accepted through faith in Jesus Christ, so even if they fall one, twenty, a thousand times—they are not cast off and rejected. Instead, Jesus, as their High Priest, intercedes for them, pleading "the mighty arguments of Calvary," so they are seen by the Father as He sees Jesus, perfect and righteous the whole time that they—through the faith and repentance that come with the new birth—maintain a saving relationship with Him.

113

29

An Adventist marriage had just crumbled because, when the wife had been a child, her father repeatedly dragged her into the bedroom and now, twenty years later, the woman—no longer able to deal with what had happened to the girl—reacted by rejecting her husband, who wept in my arms for himself, her, and their three children.

Suppose one hot afternoon, after having just had sexual intercourse with his twelve-year-old daughter, this Adventist father, overcome with guilt, got on his knees, cried out to God, repented, forsook his sin, and was truly born again.

Would God have forgiven him? Would Christ's death cover even this? Be careful of your answer, because if it's "Yes," you're saying that this incestuous child molester suddenly stood perfect (*perfect!*) and righteous before God. You're saying that this man—who an hour before was burying his flesh into that of his own scared, weeping child—would now be covered with the righteousness of Jesus Christ. You're saying that there is "therefore now no condemnation" to him, because when God views that man, He no longer sees the filthiness of his perversion and lust, but the perfect robe of Christ's sinlessness instead.

Are you saying that?

You had better, because that's the gospel, the "mystery" of God, that "he might be just, and the justifier of him which believeth in Jesus Christ" (Romans 3:26)—a pardoning love that goes beyond anything we are emotionally or rationally capable of understanding or experiencing ourselves.

But there's the other side of the equation, a side often neglected. Because for so long the pure, basic teaching of the gospel has been lost to many Seventh-day Adventists, many have struggled with any sense of surety, assurance, or hope of salvation. For them, Paul's words, "Therefore being justified by faith, we have peace with God through our Lord Jesus Christ: By whom also we have access by faith into this grace wherein we stand, and rejoice in hope of the glory of God" (Romans 5:1, 2), have been only theological statements bouncing off the hard shells of their calloused souls—not the essence of their experience with Christ.

But now, put aside the issue of salvation and look at sin from another angle: What about the devastation, the pain, and the suffering that sin—even forgiven, pardoned sin—inevitably leaves behind? It is true that this father might have been able to get on his knees and in thirty minutes (even thirty seconds?) of prayer be "perfect in Christ." But thirty minutes of prayer hasn't healed the damage caused by that sin. Even after twenty long years, the woman was a wreck, her husband devastated, and their three children's lives uprooted—all from a sin that might have been pardoned by God ten minutes after it was perpetrated!

The point is simple: You can, in an instant, be forgiven a sin that causes yourself and your loved ones a lifetime of misery, "even to the third and fourth generation" (Exodus 20:5).

Now the Bible says that "we must through much tribulation enter into the kingdom of God" (Acts 14:22)—and every Christian knows that suffering is part of redemption, part of God's hewing and refining process, the process that separates the dross from the gold. But nothing should convince us that a father dragging his twelve-year-old daughter into the bedroom (while the mother stood by and did nothing) was all part of some divine plan to help prime the little lamb and prepare her for the glories of the Elysian Fields!

Peter said, " If ye suffer for righteousness sake, happy are ye" (1 Peter 3:14), but nothing is righteous in much of our suffering. Most of us aren't Jobs, suffering for righteousness sake; we're Uriahs, bleeding to death on the battlefield because of David's lust for Bathsheba.

No doubt, whatever we have done to ourselves, or whatever others have done to us, the Lord can heal. That's not the point. The point is that suffering comes from sin, either from our own or from someone else's, and thus so much pain could be avoided if only we had a relationship with God that allowed Him to transform us and free us from the bondage of sin.

And we can. It's called the new birth.

30

From a racist jail in Alabama, Martin Luther King, Jr. wrote that men didn't need to obey any "human law not rooted in eternal and natural law."

In the *Declaration of Independence*, Thomas Jefferson proclaimed that "self-evident truths" and "unalienable rights" were based upon "the laws of nature and of nature's God."

A century before Christ, Cicero said that all civil laws must be founded in "Nature's laws" and in "universal law."

However different their contexts, premises, and conclusions, these men all appealed to "natural law," universal principles that could be derived from the rational natural order.

Clifford Goldstein

The problem with natural-law theory isn't whether natural laws exist, but rather what moral principles, if any, can be derived from them. The law of gravity can demonstrate mathematically that if you throw yourself off a twenty-story building, you'll hit the ground at a certain speed. But can those numbers, in and of themselves, show why—under the right circumstances—you shouldn't jump?

Christians study natural law from a different perspective than those who look out and see only a cold, amoral, and essentially meaningless creation.

"The ancient covenant," wrote biologist Jacques Monod, "is in pieces: man at last knows that he is alone in the unfeeling immensity of the universe, out of which he has emerged only by chance. Neither his destiny nor his duty has been written down." No wonder sociologist Peter Berger said: "There is really nothing very funny about finding oneself stranded, alone, in a remote corner of a universe bereft of human meaning—nor about the idea that this fate is the outcome of the mindless massacre that Darwin, rather euphemistically, called natural selection."

In contrast, the premise that "God is love" (1 John 4:16) is suffused with moral connotations, and the conclusions one can draw from it differ radically from what one would draw if the verse read, for instance, "God is hate."

Because Christians believe in a moral God, they

also believe in a moral universe, because God wouldn't be moral if He placed us in an amoral or, especially, an *im*moral one. A moral Creator means a moral creation. And just as God created physical laws to govern this creation, He created moral ones as well; and just as violations of those physical laws bring consequences, violations of the moral ones do too.

"And now, Israel, what doth the LORD thy God require of thee, but to fear the LORD thy God, to walk in all his ways, and to love him, and to serve the LORD thy God with all thy heart and with all thy soul, to keep the commandments of the LORD, and his statutes, which I command thee this day *for thy good?*" (Deuteronomy 10: 12, 13, emphasis supplied).

The phrase "for thy good" appears in the singular (*letov lak*). For the good of each human, individually, personally, God has given commandments that reflect the moral principles of His creation. By obeying the commandments, we remain in harmony with the principles; by disobeying, we step into moral chaos. And though the effects of disobedience might not always be immediate, or apparent—sooner or later, in one way or another, to one degree or another, we always suffer the consequences.

"The universe," wrote William James, "at those parts which our personal being constitutes, takes a turn for the worse or the better in proportion as each one of us evades or fulfills God's commands."

Clifford Goldstein

According to Scripture, though, we're programmed to evade those commands. Inherently, genetically, temperamentally—we're in dissonance with God's moral principles. We're born with natures that serve the "law of sin and death" (Romans 8:2), not the law of love and of Christ.

So, no matter how well our birth took the first time, we need to be born again. Then can God mold us, change us, and shape our characters in a way that harmonizes us with the moral principles of creation, and thus spare us much of the grief caused by our inherent disharmony with them.

When Jesus said, "I am come that they might have life, and that they might have it more abundantly" (John 10:10), He wasn't talking just about eternity, but about a new and better life, even here, even now.

31

"Man is born free," wrote *philosophe* Jean Jacques Rousseau, "but everywhere he is in chains."
Man is born free?
Nonsense.
To begin, man had no choice regarding if, when, and where he was brought into the world. Also, he had no say whatsoever concerning his parents, nationality, or race. New-born man can't walk, talk, feed himself, or control his bowels; in fact, he's so helpless that, if left to himself, he would soon die. The infant is at the complete mercy of his elders and stays that way until old enough to gain some autonomy. Meanwhile, everything—from the color of his hair, skin, and eyes, to his basic personality traits—is

heaped upon the child without his consent, approval, or knowledge, and these traits remain the rest of his life.

When hewed, molded, and formed by forces over which you have no control, when physical appearance was determined at conception, when the clay of personality is hardened by the age of three or four, all without your choice, request, or preference—call it what you want, but that's not being born free.

Man is also not born free, because he's born a sinner, condemned to death in Adam, his natural father, from the sinful nature he inherited from Adam at birth (again without any choice on the infant's part).

"Therefore as sin entered the world through one man, and death through sin, and in this way death came to all men because all sinned" (Romans 5:12, NIV).

All of which is another reason why we must be born again. Just as Adam brought us death and bondage, Christ brings us life and freedom. "Then as one man's trespass led to condemnation for all men, so one man's act of righteousness leads to acquittal and life for all men. For as by one man's disobedience many were made sinners, so by one man's obedience many will be made righteous" (Romans 5:18, RSV).

"For as in Adam all die, in Christ shall all be made alive" (1 Corinthians 15:22)—and the experience of being "made alive" in Christ, of being freed from the condemnation of our natural birth, results from the new-birth experience.

Finally, however much free will we've been given, it's exercised only in the context of sinful flesh, which limits it severely. In our natural state, we're captive to the clamors of our fallen nature. Sin's as much a part of our essence as is breathing. We have no choice: we sin because we are born sinners—and sinners, without Christ, sin. "If we say that we have no sin, we deceive ourselves, and the truth is not in us" (1 John 1:8).

No wonder Jesus said, "Everyone who commits sin is a slave to sin" (John 8:34, NIV). Thus, because we all have sinned, we all have been slaves to it. And if our sinful nature begins at birth, or even before (it comes wrapped in our DNA at conception), how can we be born free?

We can't. Instead, Rousseau's statement "Man is born free, but everywhere he is in chains" should read, "Man is born in chains, and unless 'born again,' he everywhere remains in them as well."

32

God wants to free us, not just from the legal consequences of sin, but from sin itself and the suffering it brings. That's why He promises to remake our hearts in the image of Christ, so that we no longer have to do what our sinful natures otherwise make us do at such a terrible cost to ourselves and those we love.

Who hasn't experienced the truth of Christ's words about those who commit sin being slaves to it? Who hasn't felt the helplessness of being clutched by a power greater than ourselves? Who hasn't struggled with a habit that constantly makes us fall into the things we don't want to do, mocking our so-called freedom and our determined efforts to resist, and then whispering that deep down we don't really want to stop? Who hasn't struggled with a "demon" that seems to jerk us like a pathetic wooden puppet, so that no matter how many resolutions we make, how many tears we shed, how many teeth we grit, we're overcome by the same thing again and again? In the context of unconverted souls and sin, that's not free will.

> Then said Jesus to those Jews which believed on him, "If ye continue in my word, then are ye my disciples indeed; and ye shall know the truth, and the truth shall make you free." They answered him, "We be Abraham's seed, and were never in bondage to any man: how sayest thou, Ye shall be made free?" Jesus answered them, "Verily, verily, I say unto you, whosoever committeth sin is the servant of sin. And the servant abideth not in the house for ever: ... If the Son therefore shall make you free, ye shall be free indeed" (John 8:31-36).

His words show that freedom in Christ entails more than just freedom from the *condemnation* of sin. Legal pardon isn't the immediate context of what Christ is saying here to the Jews. When the Son makes you free, Jesus said, He makes you "free indeed," and being "free indeed" includes being free, not just from the condemnation of the law, but from bondage to the acts of sin itself.

Clifford Goldstein

God doesn't justify us so that we can go on sinning with impunity. "For sin shall not have dominion over you: for ye are not under the law, but under grace. What then? shall we sin, because we are not under the law, but under grace? God forbid" (Romans 6:14, 15). God hates sin, not just for what it is, but for what it does, and so He promises that if we continue in His word, we no longer have to be in bondage to it.

Salvation has always been a package deal. When a person has surrendered to Jesus Christ enough to be justified by Him, He will automatically be surrendered enough to be sanctified as well. The death to self that leads to a new birth also leads to a new life in Christ, one in which He works within us "both to will and to do of his good pleasure" (Philippians 2:13), and His will and good pleasure is to make us "free indeed."

33

What does it mean to be "free indeed," in the context that Jesus expressed it? What should one, who has surrendered her old life to God in order to have a new one in Christ, expect regarding sin? What happens to sin in a sinner who has been born again?

In Romans 5, Paul wrote that "where sin abounded, grace did much more abound" (Romans 5:20). Then, in response to the logical question ("Shall we continue in sin that grace may abound?"), he replied:

> God forbid. How shall we, that are dead to sin, live any longer therein? Know ye not, that so many of us as were baptized into Christ

Clifford Goldstein

Jesus were baptized into his death? Therefore we are buried with him by baptism into death. . . . Knowing this, that our old man is crucified with him, that the body of sin might be destroyed, that henceforth we should not serve sin. For he that is dead is freed from sin (Romans 6:2-4, 6, 7).

This death—to self, to sin, to the old man—is what we must die in order to be born again. Verse 2 ("How shall we, that *are dead to sin . . .*") reads literally, "How shall we, who *died* to sin . . ." The verb, an aorist, points to a particular time and event completed in the past, in this case the believer's total surrender of self (death) to Christ, which led to her new birth and justification. Paul then asked whether a person who surrendered herself to Christ, to die to her old life, could therefore live any longer as a slave to sin? His answer is No, because she "that is dead is free from sin."

Paul then discussed baptism, symbol of this death, which he equated to Christ's death at Calvary. He then wrote that "our old man is *crucified* with him, that the body of sin might be destroyed, that henceforth we should *not serve sin*" (verse 6, emphasis supplied). This isn't a legal declaration lodged somewhere out in Orion; instead, for Paul, it's an existential reality, an experience in the life of the believer who has, through the power of the Holy Spirit, crucified the old nature

129

and its attendant "affections and lusts" (Galatians 5:24).

For Paul, the believer's death to sin is as real as was Christ's death in the tomb ("Know ye not, that so many of us as were baptized into Christ Jesus were baptized into his death?"), which is why he wrote, "reckon ye also yourselves to be dead indeed unto sin" (Romans 6:11). You can't be a slave to what you have died to. According to Paul, that bondage is broken; the "old" woman died when she consciously chose to participate in the death that Christ had died at the cross for her, and now that she died, she is free from the bondage of sin.

Now, what does Paul mean when he says that we are free from, or dead to, sin? As anyone ever born again can testify, there is a radical change in the life. A new birth means just that—a new birth—and a new birth means a new life. But no person who has been born again can say, in truth, that after her new birth experience she never sinned again.

To "not live any longer therein [in sin]" means, well, not to *live* any longer in sin; it doesn't mean that we don't have temptations, weaknesses, an awareness of our sinfulness, or even times when we fall. To be betrayed into sin is not the same as to live in sin, or to be a slave to it, and so a born-again Seventh-day Adventist mustn't lose hope if she still struggles with, or even succumbs to, sin.

Clifford Goldstein

When born again in 1979, I no longer *lived in sin*. I no longer lived the way I used to, in rebellion (no matter how ignorantly) against the law of God. But though I might no longer live in sin, sin still lives in me, in my sinful flesh, even after my new birth—which is why I have to surrender, moment by moment, to the power of God, especially when tempted. If not, I succumb to my fallen flesh, which remains until the second coming.

John wrote, "Whosoever is born of God doth not commit sin" (1 John 3:9), but the verb (present active indicative) indicates a continuous action, an unbroken line of activity—a radically different concept from a born-again soul who sometimes sins.

The fact that after the new birth we still sin doesn't, of course, justify sin. There's never an excuse for sin, not for a born-again Christian, not "if the Spirit of him that raised up Jesus from the dead dwell in you" (Romans 8:11), not with such promises as, "Now unto him that is able to keep you from falling, and to present you faultless before the presence of his glory with exceeding joy . . ." (Jude 24).

What good is a religion that can't stop us from doing the things that can destroy us, not just temporally—but eternally as well? Unconfessed, unforsaken sin will, ultimately, neutralize all the power of the gospel in our lives, causing us in one way or another to sever our saving relationship with Jesus Christ.

Children of the Promise

God doesn't reject us because of sin; sin—itself an act of rejection to God—causes us to reject Him. A born-again Christian who loses her soul will lose it, not because God cast her off, but because she, hardened and deceived in sin, cast off God.

This is what happened to Judas. Judas had been so deceived by his sin that Satan made Judas think that by betraying the Lord he was furthering His kingdom. The devil used Judas's sin to sever him from Christ, and he uses ours to do the same to us. For this reason, victory over sin, through the power of Christ, is so important.

If bondage to sin is inevitable in born-again Christians, Bible promises about life in Christ mean nothing. How much power is in a gospel that redeems us from sin but can't stop us from committing it? However, because there is no excuse, we need, not only a Saviour, but a mediator, which is why Christ our High Priest "maketh intercession for us" (Romans 8:34) when we do sin. His heavenly mediation is the very means by which Christ continues to forgive us our sins after we've been born again.

While the new birth doesn't guarantee that we will never sin again, it does offer not only the assurance that we're still accepted in Christ if we do, but also an experience that promises the strength not to commit (present active indicative) sin. Being aware of our sinfulness, aware of how far from the standard of holiness we are, and even sometimes falling, isn't the same as living in sin or being a slave to it, as we did, and were, before we died in Christ.

Until that death, we were "servants of sin" (Romans 6:17) and "free from righteousness" (Romans 6:20); but now, after having been buried with Christ by baptism into His death and raised to a new life in Him, we become "servants of righteousness" (verse 18), in which sin no longer forces us "to obey it in the lusts thereof" (Romans 6:12). Instead, in Christ, we're "free indeed," and what could be more free than a person with a sinful, fallen nature who is no longer enslaved by it?

It's one thing to break bonds of metal or iron wrapped around your flesh; anyone, with the right tools, can do that. It's radically another thing to break the bonds that are locked *inside* your flesh. That takes power from on high, which, of course, is why Jesus said, "Ye must be born from above."

34

There's more to the new birth than just the forgiveness of sin, and more even than freedom from bondage to it. Not only have we died to sin in Christ, but "like as Christ was raised up from the dead by the glory of the Father, even so we should walk in *newness of life*" (Romans 6:4, emphasis supplied). Not only were we buried with Him, but "we believe that we shall also *live with him*" (Romans 6:8, emphasis supplied). Not only should we reckon ourselves dead to sin, but we should reckon ourselves "*alive unto God* through Jesus Christ our Lord" (Romans 6:11, emphasis supplied).

What does it mean to be alive with Christ? If we're to live with Christ, and to have a new life through

Clifford Goldstein

Him, what happens? What should a born-again Christian, who is now "risen with Christ" (Colossians 3:1), expect in her new life?

First, to be alive unto God through Jesus Christ means that, now, available to you—personally, individually—is all that heaven offers through the life, death, and resurrection of Jesus Christ. Because of His sacrifice, the barrier, the rift, between heaven and earth caused by sin was restored, and through Christ God is able to pour out upon us the resources of heaven.

To have a new life in Christ is to experience the reality of the living God. It's not just to believe in Him (you don't have to be born again to do that), but to *know* Him through His dynamic intervention in the recesses of our soul. To be risen with Christ is to experience His ever-present work in bringing us into harmony with the principles of His creation.

To be alive in Christ is also to know God's pardoning, healing, and gracious love toward sinful, erring humans because we experience that love in our own lives. The more we learn of that love and experience it ourselves, the more we reflect it toward others. If a new life in Christ is anything at all, it's where we learn to accept other sinners as Christ has accepted us. It doesn't mean we have to like what they do, have done, or stand for (any more than God likes what we do, have done, or stand for, either), but in Christ we begin to love and forgive others as we ourselves have been loved and forgiven by Him.

To live with Christ is to look to Him and be changed by the fullness of God's love. A power, a joy, an energy comes from dwelling upon Christ's perfect character. By studying His self-denial, His humiliation, His purity, His holiness, His patience, His self-sacrificing love—something happens in us. To be alive with Christ is to be changing into His moral image by the indwelling power of the Holy Spirit working in a soul surrendered to Him.

"But we all, with open face as in a glass beholding the glory of the Lord, are changed into the same image from glory to glory, even as by the Spirit of the Lord" (2 Corinthians 3:18).

Now, these transformations don't happen immediately. They take a lifetime of hewing, molding, and refining—and some people unquestionably acquire aspects of Christ's character faster than others. But whatever our differences (for we all come to Christ with various cultivated or inherited qualities), a new life in Christ is where the words—"he that hath begun the good work in you will perform it unto the day of Jesus Christ" (Philippians 1:6)—are believed, not because we necessarily feel, see, or sense them fulfilled in us, but because God has promised and we accept that promise on faith.

To live in Him is to live by faith. It is to believe that

we're saved, to believe that God hears our prayers, to believe that He loves us, and to believe that "all things work together for good to them that love God" (Romans 8:28)—even when, at times, reason seems to scream in our ears not to believe these promises at all.

Being alive in Him is, finally, to let the heart, moved by the Spirit, take you where reason won't go. "The heart has its reasons," wrote Pascal, "which reason does not know." And what reason cannot know ("How can a man be born when he is old?" John 3:4), the heart often can—which is why the heart alone can best grasp Christ's words, "Ye must be born again" (John 3:7).

35

In Romans and Galatians, Paul distinguished between the law, which shows our need of salvation and faith in Christ, the means of appropriating salvation. Interestingly enough, Paul cited Abraham as an example of someone with this saving faith. In fact, he called Abraham the father of all who believe. "And if ye be Christ's, then are ye Abraham's seed, and heirs according to the promise" (Galatians 3:29).

Promise? What promise?

The promise of Jesus Christ and the righteousness that leads to eternal life. "And this is the promise that He has promised us, even eternal life" (1 John 2:25). When we appropriate that promise for ourselves, we become its children, children of the promise.

Clifford Goldstein

"They which are the children of the flesh, these are not the children of God; but the *children of the promise* are counted for the seed" (Romans 9:8, emphasis supplied).

In our natural state, we're the seed of our earthly fathers, children of the flesh; when born again, we're the seed of Abraham, children of God and children of the promise.

"But to all who received him, who believed in his name, he gave power to become children of God; who were born, not of blood nor of the will of the flesh nor of the will of man, but of God" (John 1:12, 13, RSV).

Paul is explicit: the promise is real only by faith, not by works of the law; in fact, the law ruins the promise. "For the promise, that he should be the heir of the world, was not to Abraham, or to his seed, through the law, but through the righteousness of faith. For if they which are of the law be heirs, faith is made void, and the promise made of none effect" (Romans 4:13, 14).

The promise becomes valid by "the righteousness of faith," which is why the new birth, the experience of "the righteousness of faith," is so crucial. We must be born again, because only then are we "children of the promise."

Now, we can't make ourselves "children of the promise" any more than we can, as Nicodemus said, enter "the second time into . . . [our] mother's womb" and be born again (John 3:4). But it will never happen without our consent, without our complete surrender to the Holy Spirit.

Perhaps, even now, the Spirit's touching you. You're feeling convicted, a prodding within? After all these years, the Lord might have brought you to this point, to this very place in *Children of the Promise*—and you now want that promise for yourself. You face a struggle; you face fears, but also a longing, a craving, a screaming for something that you don't have, but want.

Your life, especially your relationships (to God and others) aren't what they should be. You've told yourself a thousand times that you are happy, but deep down you're miserable (and know it too). You live a life of quiet desperation, and however much you long for assurance, for peace, for purpose, they never come.

You sense guilt, sin, angst, and lots of pain, but behind it all—hope. Hope because Jesus Christ is reaching out for you, to take you to Himself, to be one of His own, bought with His blood. Don't wait to *feel* His acceptance; claim it by faith, because in Jesus Christ you have assurance, forgiveness, and righteousness no matter how doubtful, guilty, and unrighteousness you are.

That's the promise!

Clifford Goldstein

But you must surrender your pathetic little existence to Him—completely, totally, unreservedly. Give Him all, and whatever is worth keeping He will, in His time, return.

If this describes you, if these thoughts are stirring within—don't wait. Fall before Him and die to all in you that is sin and self and flesh so that, in Him, you can have life and light and power. Exchange the guilt, the shame, and the past for a new life in Christ. You, you alone, have to *choose* to do it, because God will never make that decision for you.

If you claim the promise, fall before Him now and pray: *Lord, I know that I'm a wretch. I know that no good thing dwells within me. I have turned my back on You so many times. I am a slave to my flesh, and even my "good" words have been polluted with self and self-righteousness. I have squandered, I have wasted, I have abused Your blessings. I have treated others, even the ones I love, shabbily, unfairly, badly. I deserve nothing but death, condemnation, and shame. I know all these things; I acknowledge all these things; I repent of all these things; and I confess all these things. But even in the midst of all my ignominy, I cry out to You. I cry out of desperation, unworthiness, and utter wretched need. O, Lord, I don't understand how You could still accept me, but claiming Jesus Christ, and His worthiness and holiness—I surrender everything to You. My whole life, every atom, every cell, everything, I give it all, I surrender it all, I die to it all so*

Children of the Promise

that I can live in You in obedience to Your commands. Take me, please, because of Jesus; accept me, please, because of the cross; make me Your child, please, because of His death for me. I fall before the foot of the cross and choose to die with Jesus there, that I may rise and live with Him, now and forever. Please, please, take my polluted offering and accept it because of the perfect offering made in my behalf. O, Lord, hear; O, Lord, forgive; O, Lord, accept me in Jesus. I give myself to You in repentance and in full assurance that You accept me because You have fulfilled Your promise in Jesus Christ, and through Him that promise is fulfilled in me.

Surrender yourself to Christ, with all your heart, with all your soul, and with all your strength, and you will be—born again.

LIFE - IMPACTING BOOKS

Clifford Goldstein has done it again! Through biblical narratives and experiences, Goldstein has consistently introduced a bold, new look at Christian doctrines, prophecies, and practice. This best-selling author has a series of life-impacting books that will inspire and challenge you in your Christian life. You'll no doubt receive a blessing from these books. All are published by Pacific Press and are available through your Adventist Book Center.

Children of the Promise—In his latest book, author Clifford Goldstein explores the concept of "born again" and poses the startling question, "Is that something Adventists even do?" Goldstein guides us through Scripture and takes a penetrating look at Christ's promise of salvation, and how we can become "children of the promise."
Paper, 144 pages. US$8.99/Cdn$12.99.

Between the Lamb and the Lion—Takes a look at Christ's role as High Priest in the heavenly sanctuary as depicted in Revelation and answers the question, *What is Jesus doing now?*
Paper, 128 pages. US$8.99/Cdn$12.99.

False Balances—Establishes the relevance of the sanctuary and the investigative judgment to our salvation and our purpose as God's people.
Paper, 192 pages. US$8.99/Cdn$12.99.

How Dare You Judge Us, God?—A fresh insight into the unseen battle behind universal pain. Goldstein uses the book of Job to reveal the cause of our sickness and its cure. **Paper, 96 pages. US$6.99/Cdn$9.99.**

One Nation Under God—Exploration of the current state of religious liberty in America. Goldstein presents the reasoning, logic, and validity of the arguments that oppose the Seventh-day Adventist position on religious liberty. **Paper, 208 pages. US$10.99/Cdn$15.99.**

The Remnant—A passionate and sincere look at the "remnant" church and the state of doubt of its believers. *Who is the remnant? Can the remnant apostatize?* are just a few of the questions the author deals with.
Paper, 128 pages. US$8.99/Cdn$12.99.

Available at your Adventist Book Center or call toll free 1-800-765-6955.

Pacific Press Publishing Association
Creating the future of Adventist publishing
Visit us at http://www.pacificpress.com